Free & Easy
stitch style

Free & Easy
stitch style

D&C
David and Charles

www.rucraft.co.uk

A DAVID & CHARLES BOOK
Copyright © David & Charles Limited 2009

David & Charles is an F+W Media, Inc. company
4700 East Galbraith Road
Cincinnati, OH 45236

First published in the UK in 2009
First published in the US in 2009

Text copyright © Poppy Treffry 2009
Photography copyright © David & Charles 2009
Illustrations by Prudence Rogers

A catalogue record for this book is available from
the British Library.

ISBN-13: 978-0-7153-3160-6 paperback
ISBN-10: 0-7153-3160-4 paperback

Printed in China by Shenzhen Donnelley Printing Co Ltd
for David & Charles
Brunel House, Newton Abbot, Devon

Commissioning Editor: Jennifer Fox-Proverbs
Editorial Manager: Emily Pitcher
Editor: Verity Muir
Project Editor: Karen Hemingway
Senior Designer: Mia Farrant
Art Editor: Prudence Rogers
Production Controller: Kelly Smith
Photography: Lorna Yabsley

Visit our website at www.davidandcharles.co.uk

David & Charles books are available from all
good bookshops; alternatively you can contact
our Orderline on 0870 9908222 or write to us at FREEPOST
EX2 110, D&C Direct, Newton Abbot, TQ12 4ZZ (no stamp
required UK only); US customers call 800-289-0963 and
Canadian customers call 800-840-5220.

CONTENTS

Introduction

I hope this book makes you look at your sewing machine in a whole new light – not just as a maker of curtains and tablecloths, but as an artist's tool. As you work your way through the steps and become more confident with the techniques, you'll be able to make your machine do things you never thought it could!

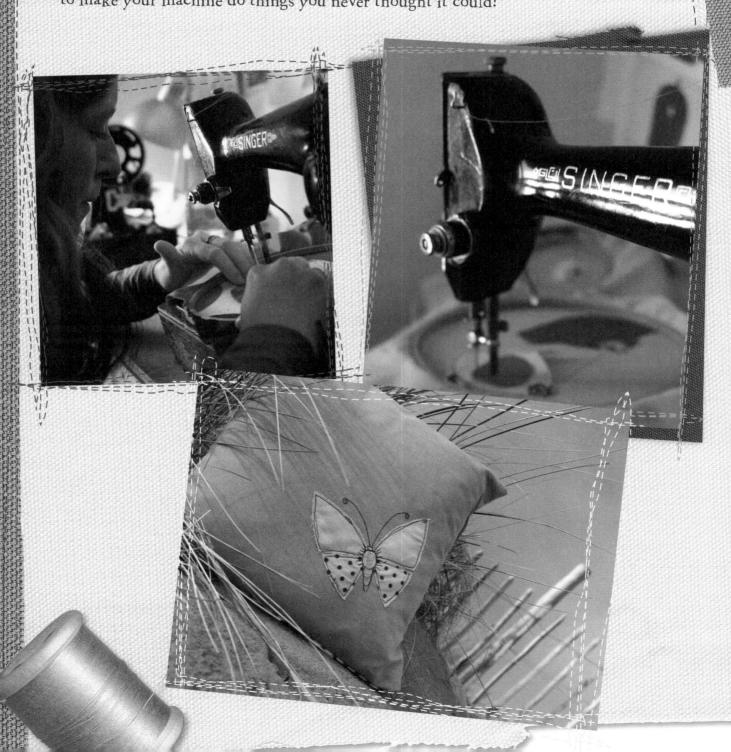

There are no hard and fast rules – in fact many of the techniques will work best if you adapt them to your own way of working and add your own creative touches. The more you push the boundaries, the more exciting your projects will become. So don't approach this book hoping for perfection – it's often the imperfections and happy accidents that help you come up with something beautiful and original.

Getting started

Basic kit

The beauty of this way of stitching is that you'll probably already have everything you need – and if you haven't got enough fabric, you'll certainly enjoy hunting out more. It's a great excuse to hoard and collect, cut up those old worn-out clothes and add in that odd little piece of ribbon or special button from your granny. That said, the list below should help to make things easier.

Sturdy sewing machine

You need to feel comfortable with your machine and get on well with it as you will be putting it through its paces. It should have a freehand embroidery function and a darning foot for free-motion embroidery, as well as a running foot for straight stitching for making up projects.

Sharp scissors

Again, good quality is essential for a pair of tailors' shears and a little pair of trimming scissors. It's important to keep them sharp – otherwise you make your work harder. So, no chopping paper with them!

Wooden embroidery hoop

It's important to spend a bit of money here and get a really good quality hoop. Cheaper hoops may damage your fabric or not hold it tightly enough. Choose the size that suits your piece of work. A 20cm (8in) hoop is a very versatile size, but it's also handy to have a small 7.5cm (3in) hoop and possibly a bigger one too.

Threads in lots of colours

Good quality polyester thread works best. Poor quality thread will snap constantly and make your life a misery, though you may get away with it for winding the bobbin. You'll need lots of colours – I love grey, black, red, orange, blue, green, cream and white.

Yummy fabric scraps

Collect lots! You want to be inspired by
your fabrics, so make sure you've got
lots of lovely little pieces hoarded for
your projects. Use scraps from previous
projects, your own old clothes or hunt
out treasures from vintage and thrift
stores. Heavy fabrics or ones with a
loose weave don't work so well, but
cotton patchwork fabrics are ideal.

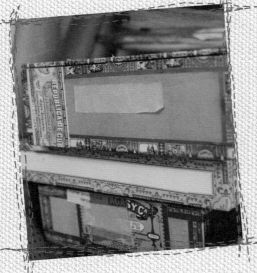

Buttons, bits and bobs

Big distinctive buttons, and other
decorative bits and bobs, are great for
giving your projects the personal touch.
Don't forget to sew them on with
strong thread! And always go for the
best quality you can afford – the better
the ingredients, the better the dish!

Templates

The templates for the projects in this
book are on pages 124–127. You will
have to scale some of them up using
paper, a ruler or tape measure, and a
pen or pencil.

Thread your machine

Of course you could just use one colour for your embroidery, but mixing two colours will give you some great effects even if you have never stitched in this way before. Two thread colours will give your stitching a more artistic quality. You can mix them to create depth, texture and interest in your work – just like mixing paints.

one Select your main colour and thread up your machine with it in the usual way.

two Select your accent colour and wind it onto the bobbin. Insert the bobbin into the machine and bring the thread up ready for sewing. Now you're ready to go.

thread contrasts with the background and complements the dots

dark stitching makes a strong statement

GOOD COLOUR COMBINATIONS

I recommend a grey top thread and black bobbin thread for getting started as they produce a nice strong line a bit like a pencil drawing. Other favourites are:

- orange top and red bobbin thread
- pink top and white bobbin thread
- blue top and green bobbin thread

shading adds
another dimension

bobbin thread adds
texture and interest

TENSION

Follow your machine manual for guidance on tension, especially if you want to keep it regular. You can also create great special effects by altering the tension. For example, tighten the tension of the top thread to let more of your accent colour come through or loosen it so that you see more of the top thread. All machines will behave differently here, so it's well worth having a play to see what your machine can do. Remember that the tension will be effected by the weight of the fabric you are using, how tightly it is stretched over your hoop, and the thickness and quality of the thread you choose. Once you find a tension setting that feels comfortable, then it's best to stick with it.

T I P It's a good idea to keep a collection of bobbins wound with different coloured threads so that you can change and play around with colours quickly and easily.

Hoop up 'n' drop the feed dog

Before you start embroidering you need to stretch your fabric in an embroidery hoop so that it doesn't pucker. The finished results depend on getting this right, so don't worry if you have to practise. The tighter you can stretch your fabric over the hoop, the better your embroidery will look.

one　Adjust the screw on the outer hoop to open it slightly.

two　Place your background fabric right side up over the outer hoop so there's the same amount of excess fabric on all sides. Position the screw on the hoop furthest away from you.

three　Position the inner hoop on top of your fabric so that it sits within the outer hoop. The fit should be tight, but not so much that you force the hoops or mark the fabric.

four　Adjust the screw on the outer hoop to make the fit tighter if necessary. You will have more success if you adjust it close to the right size before fitting the inner hoop.

five　Work your way around the hoop, holding your thumb on the top edge and gently pulling the fabric to make it as tight as it will go – a bit like a drum skin.

six　Drop the feed dog on your machine and attach the darning or embroidery foot. Place the hoop, right side up, under the needle – and you're ready to stitch…

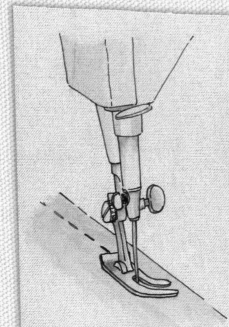

DARNING FOOT

When working free-motion embroidery techniques (see pages 14-29), fit the darning foot to your sewing machine. This will help to keep your fabric from puckering up while protecting your fingers as you move your work freely under the needle.

As a well-practiced machine embroiderer, I prefer not to use a darning foot, as you will see from the photos in this book. However, I would recommend for safety's sake that you do.

TIP Keep a pile of 30cm (12in) squares of medium-weight cotton drill ready for playing with. Don't spend too much money on the fabric – or cut up old sheets or clothes. That way you don't have to worry about being perfect first time!

FEED DOGS

The feed dog, up in its normal position, grips and feeds the fabric. When it's dropped, the fabric can be moved around freely in any direction.

Sewing machines differ, so check how to drop your feed dog in the manual. Some are controlled by a button, others by a screw.

feed dogs dropped

Techniques

Outlining

Outlining is a key technique for getting to grips with freehand machine embroidery. Imagine you are drawing with the sewing machine needle, but instead of moving the pencil you are moving the paper. This takes practice, so don't expect to be an expert right away – the more you do, the more relaxed and confident you feel, the better your work will become.

Experimenting with shapes

By keeping things simple and not expecting too much at first, you will gradually get used to the technique. Start by letting the machine guide you as you scribble and then take control a little more to create some specific shapes.

one Thread your machine and hoop up your fabric (see pages 10 and 12). Place your hoop under the needle and drop the foot. Lower the needle into the fabric. Set your machine to straight stitch and for even tension. The length of the stitch will be controlled by the speed at which you move the hoop.

two Start to sew slowly, controlling the speed carefully with your foot. At this stage don't worry about the shape, just sew some wiggly lines and scribbles just to feel comfortable with the machine. As your confidence grows, increase the speed to a steady medium pace so your stitched lines flow more smoothly.

three Next try outlining some simple shapes like squares and circles with the needle. You will get the feel for what the machine will do and realize that you can move the hoop in any direction.

four Outlining a shape a couple of times, with the inevitable crossing of stitch lines, will secure your stitching to some degree. If in doubt, finish off by sewing a few stitches backwards.

squiggles to start

double outlines look attractive

Practise will help you create shapes that look recognizable and charming.

T I P Don't be scared of making a mess! Scribble shapes on top of other shapes and play around with colours. You are just getting used to the feel of the machine, you're not creating a masterpiece – yet!

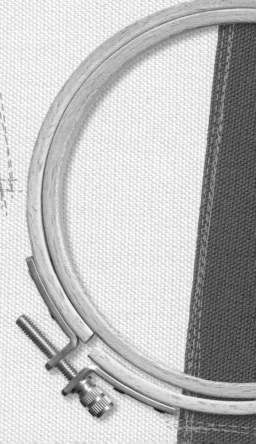

five Now try some more complicated shapes like hearts, leaves and flowers. You'll get through quite a few squares of fabric as you play around to build your confidence and feel more relaxed with the technique.

Copying an image

Once you feel more confident, have a go at working from a photograph or drawing. Place the image on the wall behind your sewing machine so that you can see it when you look up, and try copying it.

You will find that it is quite similar in some ways to drawing with a pencil – but quite different as well. You can take a pencil off the paper and move to another area; but with sewing, you have to stop the machine, remove the needle from the work and then move to your next area, cutting off the floats of thread afterwards.

Once you get more confident, you'll find you can create some really nice effects by not restarting in a new area, but by letting one line lead into another – like drawing when you're not allowed to take your pencil off the paper. You will inevitably end up with a drawing that's more childlike and scribbly – but I think that's part of the charm of the technique.

Don't worry if your outlines aren't smooth – the squiggles and overlaps add unique character to your work.

TROUBLESHOOTING

Most of the problems that you might encounter are related to tension – both of the machine and machinist! The more relaxed you become, the more smoothly things will go. It also helps to make sure your machine is clean, well oiled and free of fluff.

Don't panic! There are easy remedies to problems such as needles snapping and thread balling up in the Troubleshooting section on pages 34–35.

TIP Keep things simple – and remember that wobbly lines are a thing of beauty in the world of freestyle sewing!

Shading

Once you've got to grips with outlining, shading is the next logical step. It's used to add texture, depth and interest to your work – just as though you were drawing. It contrasts with the appliqué to add different features to your projects and is a great way to maximize the effects of mixing thread colours.

There are four ways to use shading on pages 18–21. Once you feel confident with the basics, experiment with different shapes, colours and types of stitches.

Basic shading

This technique is useful for filling in quite large areas with shading. It's simple, but can be very effective.

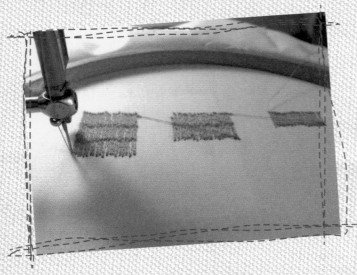

one Select your colours – one for the top thread and one for the bobbin. These could be the same colour, or you might want to try something a little jollier by using two different ones.

two Hoop up your fabric, place it under the needle and drop the foot. Lower the needle into the fabric and outline a 2.5cm (1in) square.

Overlap the rows of stitches slightly to build up your shape.

three Slowly start sewing within the square, moving the work back and forth by about 1cm (½in) to make a row of stitches across the fabric. Build up the shaded area, overlapping the rows slightly, until you have filled the square.

T I P As with drawing, shading with the machine looks best if the stitches run in the same direction.

Basic shading is used throughout the projects in this book to fill in larger areas of colour.

Shading circles

Once you've mastered shading a square, have a go at shading a circle. Sew the outline of a circle 2.5cm (1in) in diameter. Then move the work back and forth to fill in the circle with rows of stitching.

Alternatively you could start in the centre and work outwards in circles to shade the area in – like drawing a spiral.

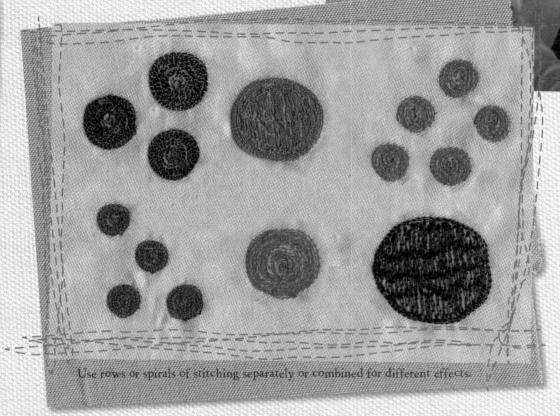

Use rows or spirals of stitching separately or combined for different effects.

Highlighting and deeper shading

Once you feel confident, try shading an area and then adding highlights in another colour combination. The easiest way to do this is simply to change the top thread. Alternatively add deeper shading with a darker thread.

Darker shading adds depth and interest, especially stitched in a different direction.

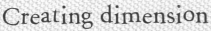

Creating dimension

You can use the shading technique to sew any three-dimensional shape just as you would with a drawing. Try creating a cube or sphere using shading to make the shapes look more solid.

T I P Practise shading with a paper and pencil first and then try to imitate your drawing with the sewing machine.

Confident shading in the right areas makes shapes distinctly three-dimensional.

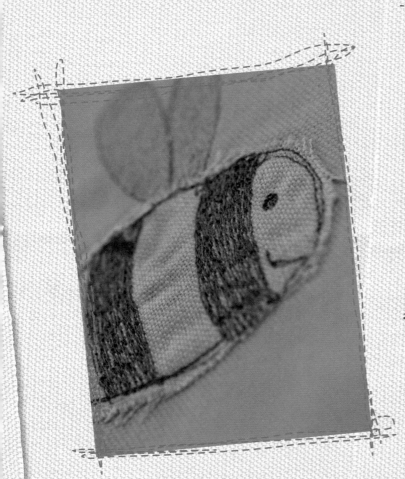

Appliqué

Think of appliqué as using fabric in place of colour and texture. If you think of your projects as drawings or paintings, you are simply replacing the paint with multicoloured, patterned and textured scraps of fabric.

For these projects, appliqué is not about being neat and tidy – it's much more about spontaneity and about finding exactly the right pieces of fabric for the job. In this section you'll find plenty of raw edges, lots of layered fabrics and many ideas for mixing fabrics together in ways you may not have imagined.

So don't worry if it takes a while to find your confidence – it's not a technique that you can perfect in five minutes!

Basic appliqué

To begin with it's best to stick to very simple exercises and easy fabrics. Try some simple template shapes like the circle, square and triangle on page 124, a medium-weight cotton drill for the background fabric and patchwork cotton, winceyette or baby cord for the appliqué.

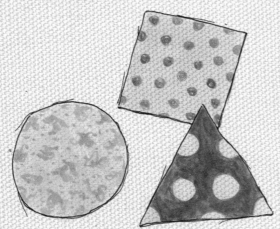

one   Cut a selection of different shapes from your appliqué fabrics, making sure that your scissors are sharp and the edges do not fray too much.

two   Place one of your shapes on your hooped-up background fabric and lower the needle into the top corner. Ideally, hold the appliqué piece in place with your fingertips so that your work keeps a lovely spontaneous look. However, if you really feel the urge to be neat and tidy, you could use a fine pin in the centre of the shape or fusible web to hold it in place.

three Slowly start to sew around the appliqué piece, moving the hoop whilst keeping the appliqué in place. Sew around the appliqué two or three times to make sure that it is really secure and can't fray too much. In general, sew a little way in from the edge – however, a wobbly line and a few scribbles can look very effective.

TIP Make a feature of your stitching by picking thread colours that contrast strongly with your appliqué fabric. For example, a pale pink or green thread looks great on a deep navy fabric and a navy thread looks great on a green or orange background.

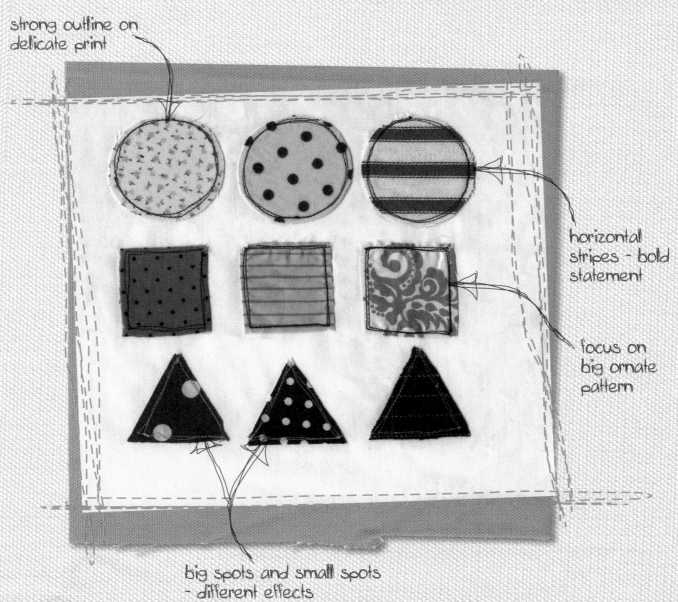

strong outline on delicate print

horizontal stripes - bold statement

focus on big ornate pattern

big spots and small spots - different effects

Shaped appliqué

Once you've mastered stitching the simple shapes, you can get started on some more complicated ones and begin to combine different fabrics.

Love hearts

A heart is quite a simple shape to stitch – but it looks really sweet.

pretty scribbles

visible weave adds texture

bobbin thread adds interest

multiple outlines

stitching emphasizes heart shape

basic layering looks sweet

Choose different patterns of fabric to give each heart its own character.

one Cut a few hearts out of different pink and red fabric scraps, using the template on page 124.

two Sew the appliqué on with contrasting thread for a pretty effect.

T I P Try a little layering and grouping of different sized hearts. You could also experiment with bringing the bobbin thread through to the surface by tightening the tension on your machine.

Funky flowers

These flowers are a little trickier to cut out and stitch, but once you get used to them they are really simple and very effective.

TIP Play with layering and grouping different sized flowers for the best arrangement before you stitch them down.

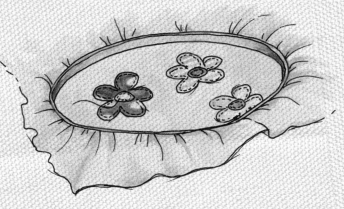

one Cut each flower out of two contrasting fabrics using the template on page 124. Choose either a dark or pale fabric for the main flower and something contrasting for the centre spot.

two Lay the main flower onto your background fabric and then position the centre spot on top. You can stitch the flowers in two contrasting threads, using dark thread on light fabric and light thread on the dark.

centre spot coordinates with petal fabric

pale thread disappears through the dots

plain and patterned fabrics contrast well

multiple layering needs planning

Contrasting thread makes the petal shapes stand out well.

Layering appliqué

Layering allows you to use two or three different fabrics to build up your embroidery. I have used it here to stitch little cup cakes, but the technique is used throughout the projects in this book.

Cup cakes

These scrummy cakes are fairly simple, but do involve three different fabrics. Select a plain fabric for the paper case, a different more striking fabric for the actual cake and then a contrast for the cherry on top.

one Cut the three shapes using the template on page 124.

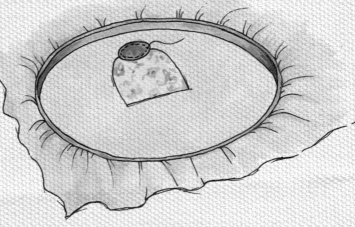

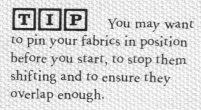

TIP You may want to pin your fabrics in position before you start, to stop them shifting and to ensure they overlap enough.

two Lay the cake fabric onto your background fabric first and then position the cherry fabric on top. Stitch the cherry on first, as it is the most likely to blow away or move – hold on to it carefully as you sew, or pin it in place.

three Then position and stitch on the paper case, adding stitches to create the fluting.

four Finally stitch around the cake fabric in a contrasting or coordinating thread colour.

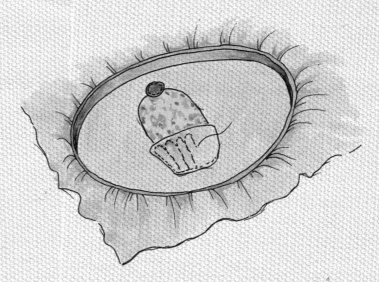

unexpected patterns - floral print for icing!

stitching detail adds flutes

the same fabric unifies the collection

Let your imagination run riot when it comes to choosing the fabrics to create the icing on the cakes.

Creative appliqué

After practising the exercises on the previous pages, you should now be feeling fairly confident about choosing fabrics, cutting out shapes and layering them, as well as stitching the pieces down. The following exercise should help you to strengthen your skills, combine them with some other techniques and be more creative.

Self-portrait

In this exercise you are going to create a stitched self-portrait! Have fun – it's just a way of practising your skills and you don't need to be Leonardo da Vinci!

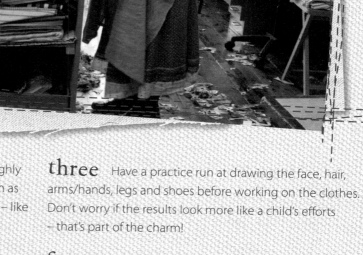

one　It will help if you draw your portrait roughly on paper first. You can then work from this sketch as you stitch. Focus on your distinguishing features – like curly hair or being very tall.

two　Have a think about your favourite clothes or an outfit that is very typical to you. Then search through your fabric scraps to find something along similar lines. Working from your sketch, cut out the different elements of your outfit. Remember you can layer fabrics, so you can place a shirt under a jacket, a skirt over a shirt and so on. It's also fun to add a handbag or a hat.

three　Have a practice run at drawing the face, hair, arms/hands, legs and shoes before working on the clothes. Don't worry if the results look more like a child's efforts – that's part of the charm!

four　Once you feel ready, place your outfit pieces onto the background fabric and stitch carefully around each one, adding the head, arms/hands, legs and shoes as you go. You can use the shading techniques too (see pages 18–21) to colour in the shoes, for example.

EXTENDED FAMILY

If you enjoyed creating your own portrait, have a go at drawing other members of your family, friends or even pets. Once you get going, there's really no reason to stop!

squiggly stitching adds detail for hair

layering

frayed edges add character

outline

fabrics that match your style

shading

Choose fabrics that say something about the real you.

TIP This is a great excuse to use some lovely vintage fabric scraps and pieces cut from your own old clothes to make up the outfits.

Dealing with edges

As you may have guessed, I am not a fan of neat and tidy! My aim is to give you the tools and skills of freehand machine embroidery and appliqué so that you can go away and create with them – in your own way. Very often it's the mistakes and experiments and deviation from the instructions that lead to the most interesting discoveries.

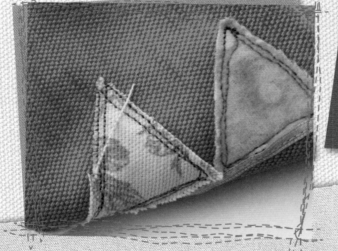

IDEAS TO TRY

- Use tighter weave fabric for smaller details such as flower petals so they don't fray away to nothing.

- Use looser weave fabrics where you want more texture, for example, for trees and bushes in a garden.

- Use the torn edge of a fabric for fraying that looks soft but uniform.

- Trim edges after you have appliquéd the fabric if they have become a bit too messy.

- Tease away weft threads after you have appliquéd the fabric to make a feature of the frayed edge.

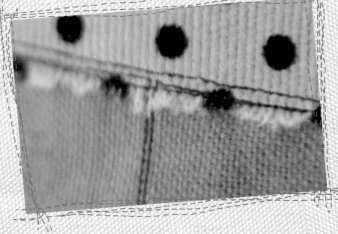

You'll see a lot of raw edges on the projects in this book. I love the different effects I can get by using different fabrics. Brushed cotton, winceyette and felt all give crisp neat edges. Cotton curtain lining, cotton poplin and fine linens give edges that fray a little and provide a lovely texture to your work. Furnishing fabrics, corduroys, denims and fabrics with a looser weave give a much more dramatic frayed edge.

TIP Practise using different types of fabric – from very closely woven winceyette to heavyweight furnishing fabrics – to get a better feel for how each one behaves.

Finishing your embroidery

It may sound obvious, but one of the key elements of producing a piece of work you can be proud of is finishing it off properly. Make sure that your embroidery is trimmed and pressed before you start using it for a particular project. Then when you turn your project the right way out, you'll feel a glow of satisfaction. You won't be able to wait to give it as a gift or use it in your own home!

First, remove your work from the hoop as carefully as possible so that you don't damage the fabric. If threads are caught, don't tug at them, but snip them carefully so the work comes away from the hoop easily.

Trimming

Very often you will end up with a complete mess of thread ends on the back and front of your work. You could cut the threads as you go, but I find it easier to trim them at the end so that I can cut them really close to the work. Cut the threads on the back of the work roughly so they won't get in your way as you sew up your project.

Pressing

Always press on the rear of your work so that the iron doesn't damage the fabric. Use as much steam as you can for the particular type of fabric to get any creases out and make your work flat.

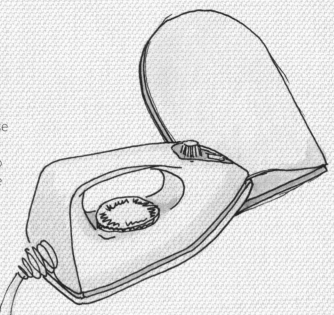

TIP If you work carefully through your project, trimming, pressing and neatening as you go, and not rushing at things and making mistakes, you will have a much more successful outcome – patience is a virtue!

Finishing projects

Instructions for making up the projects in this book appear on the project pages and there is also advice on techniques, such as mounting work to make pictures or making handles, that will be handy for many different projects on pages 42–47. For a professional finish, always trim threads and press seams flat as you go and sew the final seam to close an opening as invisibly as possible.

Troubleshooting

The techniques in this book are not meant to be learnt overnight. They take patience and practice! So don't be disheartened if you don't get them perfect right away – the important thing is to enjoy the process of learning and playing with the techniques.

That said, there are a few things that can easily be solved if they're starting to make your life difficult. The troubleshooting table below gives you a breakdown of some of the most common problems and how best to resolve them.

PROBLEM	CAUSE	SOLUTION
Needle-snapping	• Poor quality needles • Tension too tight • Lack of practice	• Always buy the best quality needles and make sure they are quite bendy. • Play with the tension to get it right – this will vary for all machines. • Practise, practise, practise!
Thread-snapping	• Poor quality thread • Tension wrong • Build up of fluff in the machine • Machine incorrectly threaded • Thread caught round spool holder	• Always use good quality thread. • Play with the tension to get it right. • Keep your machine clean and well oiled. • Check your manual to thread your machine correctly. • Gently tease out any thread that's got caught.
Thread balling up in the bobbin case	• Tension wrong • Poor quality thread • Ill-fitting bobbin • Build up of fluff in the machine	• Play with the tension to get it right. • Always use good quality thread. • Check the bobbin is in good working order and fits the machine well. • Keep the machine clean and well oiled.
Embroidery is uneven and skips stitches	• Machine incorrectly threaded • Needle wrong way round • Tension wrong • Unsuitable fabric • Poor quality thread	• Check your manual to thread your machine and insert the needle correctly. • Play with the tension to get it right. • Try using a different fabric and see if things improve. • Always use good quality thread.
Hoop leaves a strong crease on the fabric	• Hoop is too tight • Unsuitable fabric	• Ensure your hoop holds the fabric tightly without forcing the hoops together. • Try different fabrics to see how they behave.

TOP TIPS FOR ENJOYING FREEHAND MACHINE EMBROIDERY

- Relax! Everything flows much better when you feel at one with the world and your sewing machine.

- Make sure you have a comfy chair and a good sewing position.

- Be inspired by your surroundings – make your workroom a place of sanctuary.

- Be inspired by your materials – treat yourself to some lovely fabrics that you can't wait to work with.

- Add personal touches, using a favourite old shirt that's worn out or a special button that means something to you.

- It's worth spending money on good quality equipment. Cheap tools will just break or damage your work and make your life miserable!

- When everything goes wrong, take a break. Things usually look much better after coffee and cake.

- Get inspired by other artists. Do some research online, visit local galleries and craft shows, and check out magazines like *Selvedge* and *Crafts*.

- Keep things simple!

- Remember how clever you are and how impressed your friends will be when they see your handmade creations!

Fabrics

Choosing fabrics

Choosing fabrics for your projects is probably the best bit about getting started!

Before you make your final choice and go cutting into the fabric, don't forget there are several things to consider – so check out the list below. And remember the golden rule – to use the best quality you can find and afford.

Whatever your needs and favourites, it helps to have a good stash of scraps and access to a reliable fabric store so that you have plenty of choice.

GENERAL TIPS FOR CHOOSING THE RIGHT FABRIC

- Is the fabric for the background, the appliqué or other parts of the project? You might need to consider several different types of fabric depending on the purpose.

- Will the project need to be washed? Wash a scrap of fabric to make sure it's colourfast, doesn't shrink and presses well.

- Will the project take some knocks? A more hardwearing fabric will be best.

- Is the fabric for a picture or greetings card? A more delicate fabric will be fine.

Background fabrics

These will generally be plain and medium- to heavyweight fabrics. Natural fibres such as cotton, linen and wool make great background fabrics as they provide a stable base. The best place to find suitable fabrics will probably be the furnishing section of the fabric store.

Project fabrics

Choose the fabric to suit the project. For example, an evening bag will look very glamorous in light, luxurious fabrics. On the other hand, a shopping bag will need a hardwearing, medium- to heavyweight fabric such as cotton, linen, corduroy and tweed (make sure the fabric isn't too thick, though, so that it doesn't make the seams too bulky). You could also add another dimension by choosing colours and patterns to complement or contrast with the main background fabric.

TIP To inspire me in my work, I keep my fabrics in three grades – tiny precious scraps for project details, small pieces for appliqué arranged into piles of dots, stripes, flowers and plains, and lovely piles of larger pieces of background fabrics arranged by colour.

Appliqué fabrics

This is where you can have the most fun – using all your old scraps, cutting up worn-out old clothes and collecting bits from friends and family. By using vintage and used scraps, you can make your work more original and personal. Of course, you can also buy small amounts of fabric especially for your projects, and most patchwork fabrics and a lot of dress fabrics are perfect for the job.

It's best to stick to natural, medium-weight fabrics. Synthetic fabrics may stretch when you are stitching into them or melt when ironed. If your fabric is too transparent, you may be able to see too much of your background fabric underneath and this may spoil the effect. If it is too thick or too flimsy, it will be difficult to work with.

Test whether the fabric will fray. A little bit of fraying gives a nice effect (see page 30), but too much and the fabric becomes unworkable. Consider the size of the pattern on your fabric. Big patterns will not work so well once the fabric is cut out for appliqué, so it's better to choose fabrics with small-scale patterns.

Enjoy building up your collection and, if you can get away with it, make sure that you have somewhere to display your finds. I know my fabric collection is what inspires me to keep on sewing and I hope yours will do the same for you. Happy hunting!

TIP Put the word out that you are building up a fabric collection and you'll be amazed at the number of fab scraps that come your way – they may not all be usable, but there are bound to be some gems amongst them. Let your fabric shop know too as they will often have piles of remnants to sell you at very reasonable prices.

Projects

As long as everything has gone to plan, you will now be feeling relaxed and confident with your embroidery skills and happy choosing your appliqué fabrics. So this is the section of the book where you can put your skills to work and produce beautiful projects for you, your home and your friends.

Making up the projects

Once you've created a beautiful piece of embroidery, you'll want to use it on a project that looks equally professional. Follow the advice here to make sure you get the details just right. For the perfect finishing touch, you could add your signature or make a pretty label for your work.

Using the templates

All the templates you need for the projects appear on pages 124–127, where you will also find plenty of ideas for motifs to appliqué. You will need to enlarge some of the templates. The easiest way to do this may be on a photocopier, but if you don't have one of those handy you can make the same enlargements using paper, a pencil and a ruler.

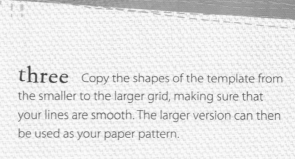

one   Trace the relevant template from the book and then draw a square or rectangle around it. Divide the outline shape up at regular intervals and draw in the lines to create a grid over the template.

two   Draw another square or rectangle on another sheet of paper, increasing the size by the factor advised. Divide up the shape with the same number of grid squares as on your smaller version.

three   Copy the shapes of the template from the smaller to the larger grid, making sure that your lines are smooth. The larger version can then be used as your paper pattern.

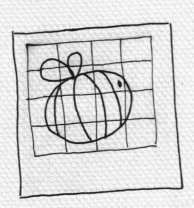

Making seam allowances

A seam allowance of 1cm (½in) can be used on all the projects, and this has been allowed for on the project templates. Of course, you don't need to think about seam allowances for the appliqué motifs!

Stretching embroidery over card

Perhaps the simplest way to display your talents is to frame your beautiful appliqué as a picture (see pages 54–59). Choose a good quality, medium-weight white card – like mount board – so that your work doesn't buckle.

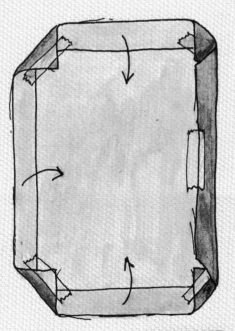

one Trim any thread ends and press your work. Cut the card to fit into the rebate of your chosen frame, with a little tolerance to allow the fabric to fit too.

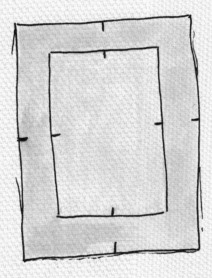

two Make sure that the fabric is thoroughly dry and place it right side down on a flat surface. Mark the centre points along each edge of the fabric and along each edge of the card. Place the card centrally on top of the fabric, aligning each pair of marks.

three Turn the corners of the fabric over the corners of the card and fix them down with adhesive tape. Then turn the edges of the fabric over the card and secure them in place with the tape, making sure that the fabric on the front of the card is taut.

four Check the effect on the right side of the picture, then choose a mount if you wish and frame up your work.

T I P Don't try to stretch your fabric too tight as it will buckle the card.

Trimming seam corners

When you have got layers of fabric, the seams can be bulky, especially at the corners. The following technique will reduce that bulk quickly and simply, making projects like the cushions look more svelte.

After you have sewn your seam, cut across the corner at a 45-degree angle with a sharp pair of shears. Cut reasonably close to the stitching, but not so close that the fabric will fray at the corner when it is turned right side out.

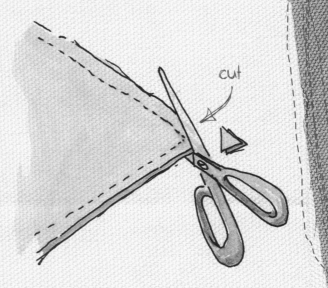

Mitring borders

The picnic blanket and matching napkins (see page 100–105) have contrasting borders that really enhance the finished projects.

TIP When you turn your work the right side out, ensure that all the corners are fully pushed out. You can do this with your finger, the end of a paintbrush or any other blunt point that you can wriggle into the corners.

one Sew the borders to all four edges of your project. Make sure that you stitch only to the point where two borders meet at each corner and that there is excess border of at least the width of the border at both ends.

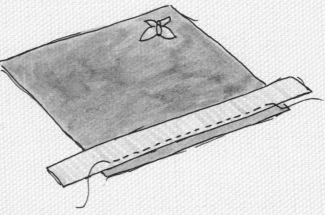

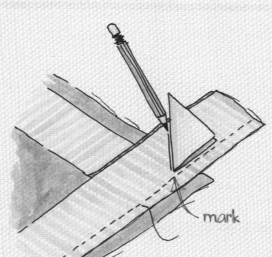

two With right sides still facing, fold one border end back on itself at a 45-degree angle. Lay the other piece of border at the same corner over the top of the first, aligning the edges and right sides facing. Mark a new seam line from the end of the existing seam at a 45-degree angle. Mark and pin the mitres for the other three corners.

three Sew all four of the new mitre seams, taking care to end each seam at the point where the previous seams meet. Trim the seams of excess fabric. Open out the borders and press all the seams.

$\boxed{T}\boxed{I}\boxed{P}$ This technique may take a little practice, so have a go using some less precious fabric first until you feel confident that you have got it right.

Making fabric loops

Little loops made of fabric can be incredibly useful. You can make them from scraps of fabric so don't buy tape specially. They are perfect for hanging up projects like the breakfast cosies (see pages 72–79) and for making buttoned fastenings.

one Cut a length of fabric about 5cm (2in) wide (you can adapt the width to suit the project or button). Fold the fabric in half lengthways and press.

two Open the fabric out, right side down, and fold each long edge over to meet along the original fold. Press the new folds.

fold

three Fold the fabric along the original line again, encasing the long raw edges. Sew neatly along both long edges.

T I P Make a much longer strip than you need and just cut off lengths as and when you need them. It saves fiddling around with shorter lengths for individual loops.

Making handles

A good sturdy handle is essential for the doorstop project (see pages 106–111), but you could also use this method to make handles for your shopping bag (see pages 80–85). Use a fabric that is hardwearing, but not too bulky – the fabric is folded so many times it can easily get too thick to work with.

one Cut a strip of fabric for the handle. A strip 20 x 7.5cm (8 x 3in) is suitable for the doorstop, but adapt the size to suit your project.

two Fold and press the ends of the strip to the wrong side. Then fold the strip lengthways to encase the long edges as described for fabric loops (see pages 45–46).

three Sew around all four edges of the fabric strip. Sew the ends of the handle in position on the project, by stitching a square and then a diagonal cross within it.

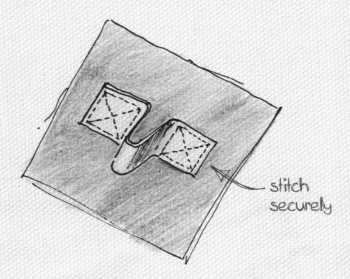

stitch securely

Personalizing your designs

Your designs will be very personal anyway, but you could add that extra special touch with a tiny motif on the back of your project or your signature. Using your sewing machine to sign your name might seem daunting, but practice makes perfect!

I sign everything I make and my signature was very wobbly at first – it's still pretty scribbly, but I think that's part of the charm. If you find writing too tricky, you could try adding a little motif such as a flower or smiley face.

Making a swing tag

Use good quality cardboard and coloured ribbon to make a very unique swing tag. You could design it on your computer, draw each one individually or photocopy an image onto card. You can also buy very attractive plain gift tags, which you could customize.

47

special greetings cards

Although you can buy every sort of greetings card in the shops these days, nothing beats making your own. In an increasingly throwaway world, it's always a pleasure to receive something that you know has taken time, care and effort to make – and very often it's much nicer than anything you can find on the shelves.

These cards are designed to be easy to make, but look like they took you a long time! Pick lighter weight fabrics in pretty colours and patterns that go well together. Also think about adding a personal touch – you could sew on some gorgeous buttons or include fabric that has special significance to the recipient.

thinking of you...wish you were here...

gather...

• Medium or lightweight background fabric
• Fabric for your chosen appliqué design
• Threads in various colours
• Good quality medium-weight card

one Use the ruler and knife on a cutting board to cut your card to the size you want. Remember the size of the finished card will be a little larger once the fabric is sewn on. Score the card down the centre line and fold. Cut and fold another piece of card fractionally smaller all round to make the inside of your card.

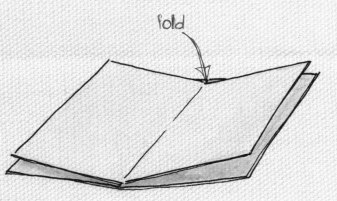

fold

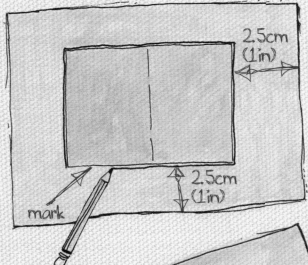

2.5cm (1in)

2.5cm (1in)

mark

two Place the larger piece of card on the wrong side of your chosen background fabric and mark around it. Cut out the fabric, adding a 2.5cm (1in) allowance all the way around. Mark a line down the middle to show where the centre fold will be.

three You can now decorate your background fabric. For the butterfly design, first add colour and pattern by sewing a panel across the bottom of the background fabric, using straight stitch. Cut out the fabrics for your chosen appliqué design, using the templates at the back of the book (see page 124 for the butterfly). Use the lines you drew on the wrong side of the fabric to ensure your motifs are in the right place.

T I P As your cards are not going to be washed or handled a lot, you can use more delicate fabrics. You also don't need to worry about making sure that the fabric edges don't fray too much.

four Using the outlining technique (see pages 14–15), stitch around the pieces of fabric for the motif. Then add the detail for the butterfly's body and antennae using the shading technique (see pages 18–19). Trim the threads and press the finished appliqué.

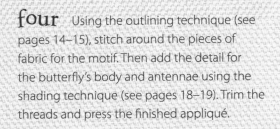

five Place the appliquéd fabric right side down with the larger piece of card centred on top. With the iron on a cool setting suitable for card, press first the corners and then the sides of the fabric snugly over the edges of the card.

T I P Sew your card together, using contrasting colours for your top and bobbin threads, to add detail.

six Centre the smaller piece of card on top so that it sandwiches the fabric edges. Then carefully machine stitch around the entire outer edge of the inner card to secure it and hide the edges of the fabric. Make sure you sew an even distance from the edge so that the stitch line looks good on the outside of your card.

FRESH AS A DAISY

The daisy card is a really pretty way of showing off your embroidery. The daisies look very ornate, but they are actually very simple to do. First stitch the yellow centre in place on top of white fabric and then work your way around looping your stitched line to create the petals. It doesn't matter if the petals are uneven or overlap as this just makes them more realistic. You can add the stems either with freehand embroidery as shown or by changing to the running foot and using straight stitch (as seen on page 122). The bumblebee is made of yellow fabric with dark shading for stripes and pale shading for its wings.

PROFESSIONAL TOUCHES

Extra special attention to detail – such as adding a signature or little motif on the back of the card – is sure to surprise and give even more pleasure.

picture perfect

How many times have you looked at a piece of art and thought 'I could do that...' or 'I wish I could do that...'? Well now there is no excuse – the easy steps on the following pages will guide you through techniques and ideas to create your own small, but perfectly formed masterpieces.

This project starts with simple ideas to build your confidence as a stitcher and bring out the artist in you. Once you have mastered your machine, there is really no reason to stick to the rules. Take the ideas and play with them, adding your own touches and finishing your artworks off with fabulous frames.

as pretty as a picture...

gather...

- Background fabric
- Fabric for your chosen appliqué design
- Threads in various colours
- Good quality heavyweight card
- Masking tape
- A mount to fit the picture frame
- A picture frame to fit the design

one Cut the card to fit into the rebate of your chosen frame. Cut the background fabric to at least 2.5cm (1in) bigger all around the card. Choose your appliqué design, starting with something simple. Make sure that it fits in your embroidery hoop and any mount you might want to use.

T I P Add a personal touch by using fabrics from favourite old clothes or by incorporating photos. As your pictures don't have to go through the washing machine, you can really add anything you like!

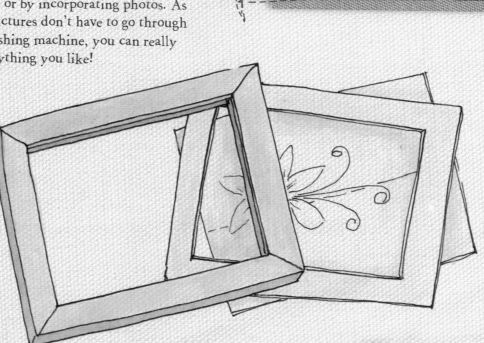

BEE INSPIRED

You can find inspiration in all sorts of places. That said don't complicate things by picking fiddly, detailed designs. This cute bumblebee is really simple but looks lovely and exploits the patterns of the fabrics used in the appliqué. Try looking at children's books, greetings cards, magazines or on the internet to find images you like. You could keep a scrapbook of cuttings of designs and illustrations that inspire you. Or follow my example and find a big wall where you can stick all the images up to get your creative juices flowing as you work.

two Cut out the fabric pieces for your appliqué design. For the lily picture, I chose a flowery print to go across the bottom half to give the impression of a summer meadow. You'll find the template for the lily petal on page 125, so have fun choosing a striking fabric for that. Cut out five petals.

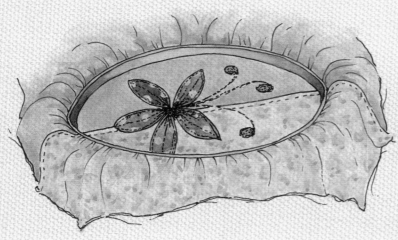

three Start by sewing the strip of fabric across the bottom half of the picture, using straight stitch. Experiment with the position of the flower and then outline the petals two or three times (see pages 14–15), using a contrasting colour of thread. Add a little shading to give depth where the petals meet (see pages 18–19). Add the stamen and outline of the stigma, using a thread colour that contrasts well with the background, with the same outlining technique. Then shade in the stigma, choosing a pretty accent colour.

T I P Some people like a picture to have glass over it as it protects the work and can look more professional. But textiles are so lovely and tactile, you might want to leave the glass out – and then you can really go to town with texture and add buttons, beads and other mementos.

four Once your appliqué is finished, trim the threads and press the fabric. Neatly stretch the finished design over the card (see page 43). Pop your picture into the frame, bang in a picture hook – and sit back and admire!

HOME IS WHERE THE HEART IS

Your pictures can be inspired by anything you love – so your
own home, or dream home, is perfect. Make notes or a sketch
of what gives your house its character – pretty windowboxes,
a red front door, a distinctive door knocker – they'll all capture
its essence. Build up the picture, adding stitched details on top
of fabrics that really represent the different parts of the house
well until you are happy.

happy days book cover

This project was especially designed to help grown-ups who want to read Harry Potter on the train without getting caught! A lovely handmade book cover will make people wonder at how clever you are, rather than wonder what you're reading. If you don't need to be secretive, package up happy photo memories or adapt your design for a diary or notebook – the perfect gift for someone deserving of your hard work!

Inspiration for your book cover could come from a holiday, a great friend or even a pet. Once you've mastered the construction, you could make a beautiful baby book or a romantic wedding album for your most treasured memories.

a book at bedtime...memories are made of this

gather...

- Background fabric (2.5cm (1in) bigger all around than the book)
- Lining fabric (size as above)
- Fabric for your chosen appliqué design
- Book or album to be covered
- Threads in various colours

one Measure the height of the book you want to cover and then the width of the book, from the front edge around the spine to the back edge. Use these measurements to make a rectangular template.

two Add 2.5cm (1in) for turning allowances at the top and bottom of the template. Add half the book's width to make pockets for the book cover at each short end of the template. Carefully cut along the lines of each rectangle.

three Use the outer edges of the larger template to cut out one rectangle of your background fabric and another rectangle of lining the same size.

cut

four Place the larger template on the wrong side of the background fabric and draw the inner rectangle onto the fabric. Press fold lines into the background fabric to help you get your design in the right place.

mark

T I P Avoid fabric that is too thick as the seams will be very bulky and the cover will not fold well round the book. Choose darker fabrics for frequently-handled books.

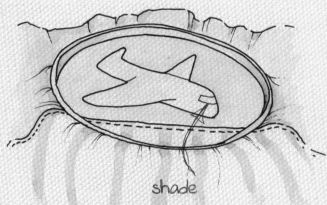

shade

five Cut out the fabric for your chosen appliqué design. For the holiday book, the template for the aeroplane is on page 125.

six First, use straight stitch to attach a panel of fabric across the bottom of the cover. Then outline the aeroplane shape (see pages 14–15). Add detail to the aeroplane by shading areas for the windows (see pages 18–19). Trim and press your appliqué when it's complete.

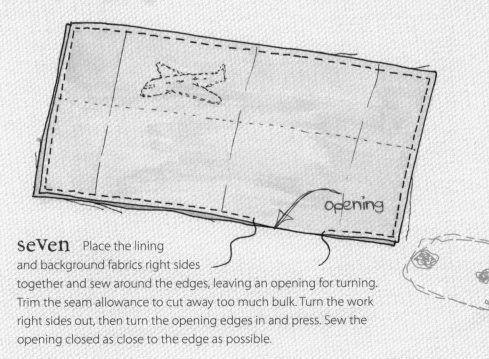

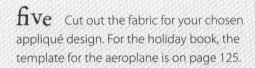

opening

seven Place the lining and background fabrics right sides together and sew around the edges, leaving an opening for turning. Trim the seam allowance to cut away too much bulk. Turn the work right sides out, then turn the opening edges in and press. Sew the opening closed as close to the edge as possible.

eight Wrap the cover around your book and close it. Carefully mark where the flaps fold in, then remove the book and press the flaps in position.

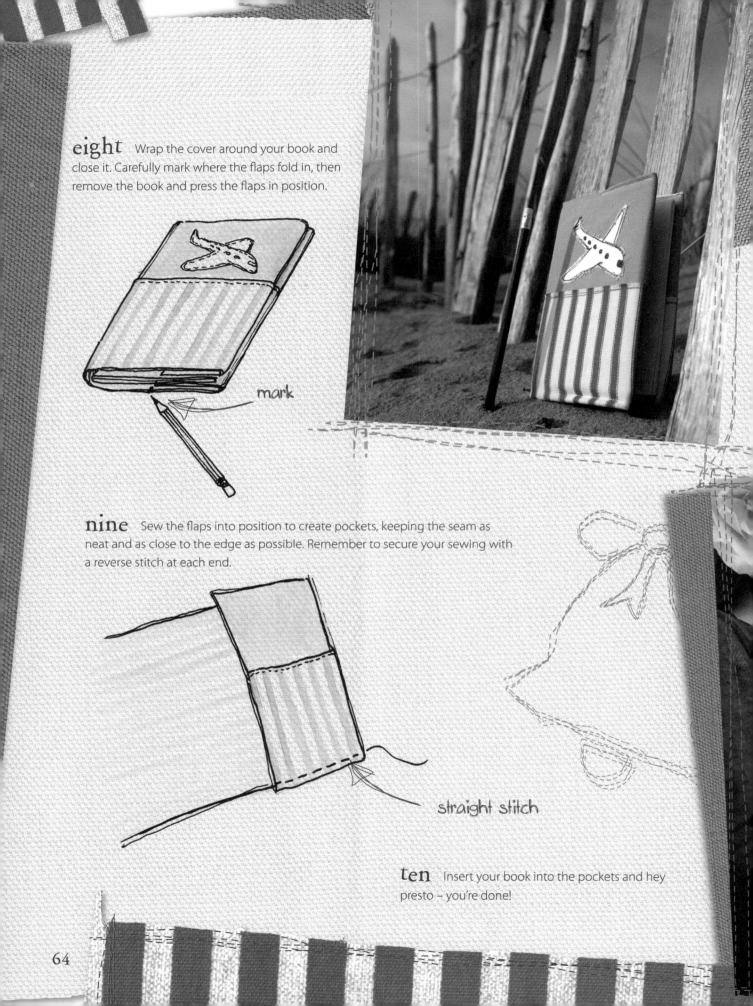

mark

nine Sew the flaps into position to create pockets, keeping the seam as neat and as close to the edge as possible. Remember to secure your sewing with a reverse stitch at each end.

straight stitch

ten Insert your book into the pockets and hey presto – you're done!

WEDDING BELLS

Capture the events of a perfect wedding day in an album steeped in memories. For the cover, you could choose fabrics that complement the theme of the day or offcuts from the bridesmaid dresses or the reception tablecloths. The bell and bow motifs can be found on pages 124 and 125.

whimsical wall tidy

So a tidy desk indicates a tidy mind, does it? I'm not sure I agree – I like my desk messy! But this wall tidy could definitely persuade me to make a place for everything. I've suggested a fruit 'n' veg theme as it makes a great way to store the endless bits of paper that clutter up the kitchen, from utility bills to the 'I'll make it one day' recipe cuttings.

Again this project looks like it took loads of work and bucketfuls of skill, but it is really quite simple and the idea is easy to adapt. It would make a great addition to a child's bedroom, and you could use nursery rhymes as your appliqué theme.

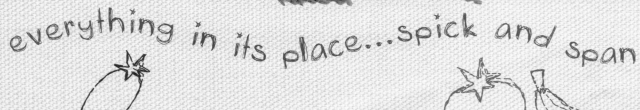

everything in its place...spick and span

gather...

- 80 x 60cm (32 x 24in) of background fabric
- 80 x 60cm (32 x 24in) of backing fabric
- 20 x 20cm (8 x 8in) x 6 of pocket fabric
- 20 x 20cm (8 x 8in) x 6 of pocket lining fabric
- Fabrics for your chosen appliqué designs
- Threads in various colours
- 45cm (18in) of tape or ribbon in a complementary colour

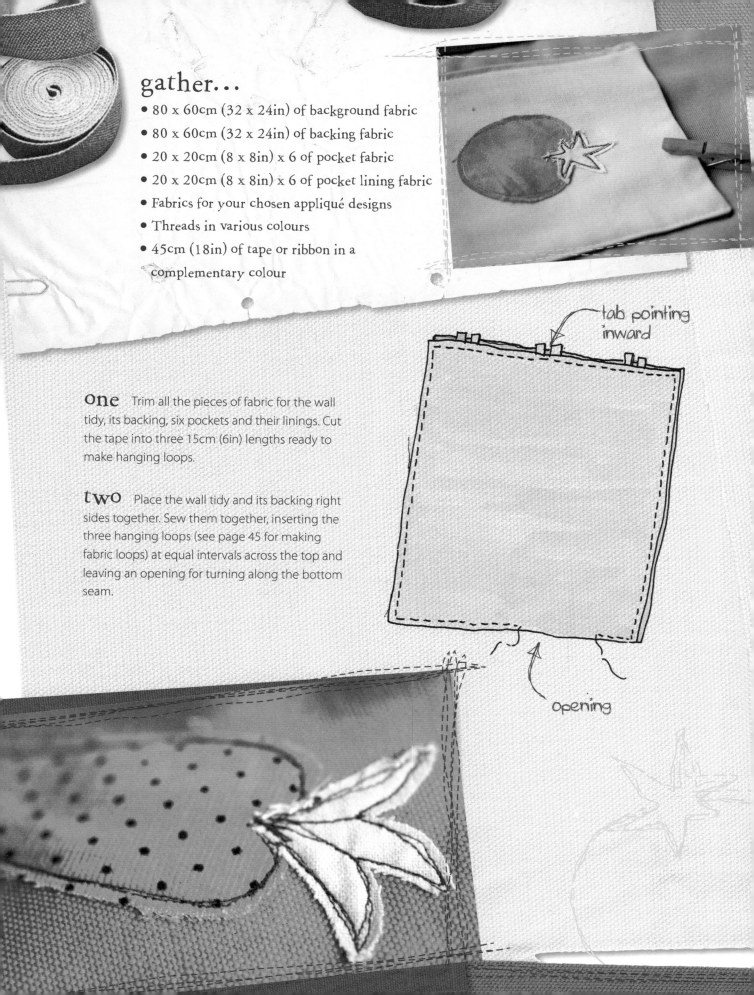

tab pointing inward

one Trim all the pieces of fabric for the wall tidy, its backing, six pockets and their linings. Cut the tape into three 15cm (6in) lengths ready to make hanging loops.

two Place the wall tidy and its backing right sides together. Sew them together, inserting the three hanging loops (see page 45 for making fabric loops) at equal intervals across the top and leaving an opening for turning along the bottom seam.

opening

three   Trim the seams to minimize bulk and then turn the fabric right sides out. Turn the opening edges in and press them in place. Stitch the opening neatly closed with matching thread.

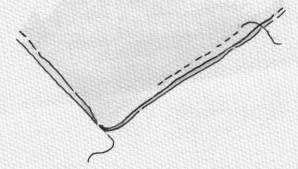

four   Cut out the fabric pieces for your chosen appliqué design, choosing the fruit and vegetable templates from page 125 or making your own up. Sew the appliqué in place by outlining the shapes onto the squares of fabric for the pockets (see pages 14–15). You could add ribs to the banana and any other detailing you think makes the objects look more charming. When the appliqué is finished, trim the threads and press each pocket piece.

T I P When choosing your appliqué design, think about what your wall tidy will be used for. It could be an ABC tidy for your child's bedroom or a handy kitchen tidy. Make up your own designs to suit your purpose.

five Sew each pocket front to its lining in the same way as you did for the main tidy, remembering to leave an opening for turning. Turn right sides out. Press them flat. You can sew the openings closed when you sew the pockets on to the tidy.

six Lay the pockets out on the wall tidy and pin them in position. Remember that some contents will stick out of the pockets, so allow plenty space above each row and position the pockets nearer the bottom than the top of the tidy.

lots of space

seven Sew each pocket in place, ensuring that your stitching is secured with reverse stitch and neatly closes the opening along the bottom edge.

eight Fill your wall tidy with stuff and then get cracking on making another one!

70

beautiful breakfast cosies

If, in some other dimension, I were to have a fabulous husband who brought me the finest ever breakfast in bed, then it would have to include these gorgeous cosies. With a cute tiny cosy to keep my boiled egg warm and a fab coffee cosy to keep my extra strong coffee nice and toasty, all I would have to do is relax and enjoy.

Failing that, of course, you can always make your own – and with these simple steps, it should be easy and fun to transform breakfast time. I have shown a few simple designs here, but you could always add some personal touches with family names and loving messages.

eggstra special...go to work on an egg

for the coffee cosy, gather...

- 40 x 30cm (16 x 12in) of background fabric
- 40 x 30cm (16 x 12in) of lining fabric
- 40 x 30cm (16 x 12in) of quilted wadding
- Scraps of fabric to make fabric loops
- Fabrics for your chosen appliqué design
- Threads in various colours

one   Make a paper pattern using the coffee cosy template on page 126 or adapting the shape to fit your own coffee pot. Use the pattern to cut out two pieces each of background and lining fabric.

two   Cut out the fabric pieces of your chosen appliqué design, using the three templates on page 126 for the coffee cup if you wish. Hoop up one piece of background fabric and stitch on your appliqué pieces, outlining each piece (see pages 14–15) and adding the handle. Use shading to fill in the coffee and the colour of the handle.

tab pointing inward

shade

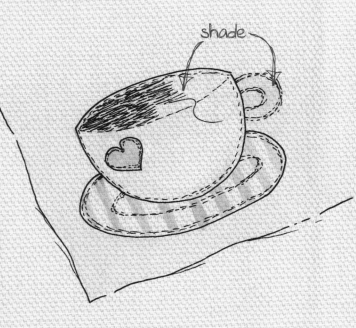

three   Press a 2.5cm (1in) turning along the bottom edge of each piece of background fabric. Make a fabric loop in a complementary fabric (see page 45). Sew the two pieces of background fabric right sides facing, remembering to insert the fabric loop at the top. Turn right sides out and press.

four Press a 2.5cm (1in) turning along the bottom edge of each piece of lining. Cut two pieces of wadding to match the lining with the turnings folded up. Place one piece of wadding right side down, then the two pieces of lining, right sides together, on top. Place the second piece of wadding, right side up, on the lining. Tuck the wadding under the turned-up edges.

fold

T I P

The cosy lining is as important as the outer fabric; make sure you show it off by allowing around 3mm (⅛in) to show at the bottom when you sew the outer and inner pieces together.

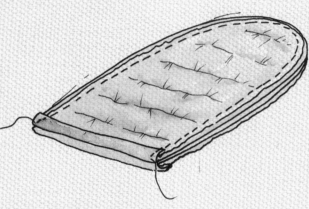

five Sew the wadding and lining sandwich together, making sure it will be the same size as the outer cosy. Use the outer cosy as a template to mark the seam lines. Trim away any excess wadding.

six Slide the wadding and lining sandwich inside the outer cosy. Open out the seams at the bottom corners and sew the lining to the outer cosy, matching the seams and leaving a little of the lining showing. Now you can put the kettle on and make a nice pot of coffee…

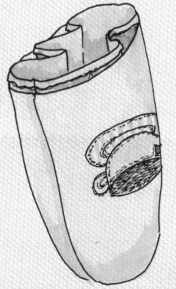

for each egg cosy, gather...

- 10 x 25cm (4 x 10in) of background fabric
- 10 x 25cm (4 x 10in) of lining fabric
- Scraps of fabric to make a fabric loop
- Threads in various colours

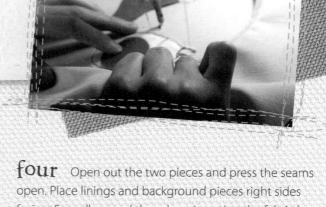

one Make a paper pattern using the egg cosy template on page 126 and use it to cut out two pieces of both background and lining fabric. Make a fabric loop to complement the other fabrics.

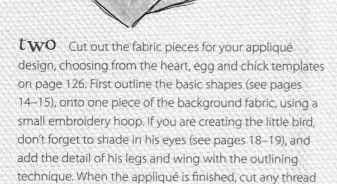

two Cut out the fabric pieces for your appliqué design, choosing from the heart, egg and chick templates on page 126. First outline the basic shapes (see pages 14–15), onto one piece of the background fabric, using a small embroidery hoop. If you are creating the little bird, don't forget to shade in his eyes (see pages 18–19), and add the detail of his legs and wing with the outlining technique. When the appliqué is finished, cut any thread ends and press the fabric.

three Place one piece of background fabric right sides facing one piece of lining and stitch along the bottom edge. Repeat with the other two pieces.

four Open out the two pieces and press the seams open. Place linings and background pieces right sides facing. Sew all around the edges, inserting the fabric loop at the top of the background fabric. Leave an opening in the lining fabric long enough to turn the fabrics through.

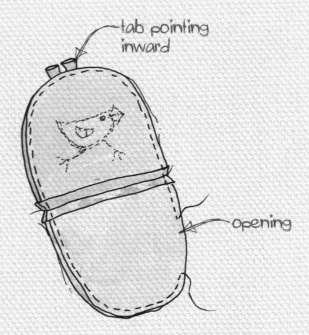

tab pointing inward

opening

five Turn the cosy right sides out and sew along the opening in the lining to close. Press the seams. Tuck the lining into the outer cosy and your egg will be just that – nice and cosy!

ONE FOR ALL THE FAMILY

Choose a different design or colourway to make an egg cosy
for everyone in the family so there are no arguments over the
breakfast table. Both the egg and heart designs look lovely in
fabrics that really make them sing.

i-love-shopping bag

This spring-like shopping bag will make you feel much better about going out for the groceries and the fact that you made it yourself will make you the envy of all your friends. Designed to look pretty and girlie, this bag also holds loads of stuff and is thoroughly practical too.

It's best to choose hardwearing, washable fabric for this bag. A canvas or cotton drill is ideal for the outer bag and, if you choose a dark colour for the lining, it will last longer between washes. The bag shouldn't be too tricky to make and will quickly become an everyday companion.

shop 'til you drop...

gather...

- 60 x 80cm (24 x 32in) x 2 of medium-weight canvas or cotton drill
- 60 x 80cm (24 x 32in) x 2 of cotton lining
- Fabric for your chosen appliqué design
- Threads in various colours
- 1.2m (1⅓yd) of tape for handles

one Trim the lining fabric to shape. Fold the fabric in half widthways. Mark 5cm (2in) in from each side edge along the top edge. Draw a line from each mark to the corner below. Cut along the lines and repeat to the second piece of fabric.

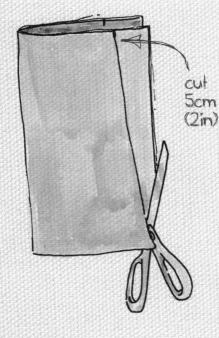

cut 5cm (2in)

two Cut out the pieces of fabric for your appliqué design, using the flower template on page 124 if you wish. Plan out and then apply the design to one piece of the background fabric.

three Use a small hoop to embroider on the flowers individually. Outline the petals and flower centres (see pages 14–15). Change to the running foot and use straight stitch in a contrasting colour to create the stems of your flowers. Trim the thread ends and press the embroidery.

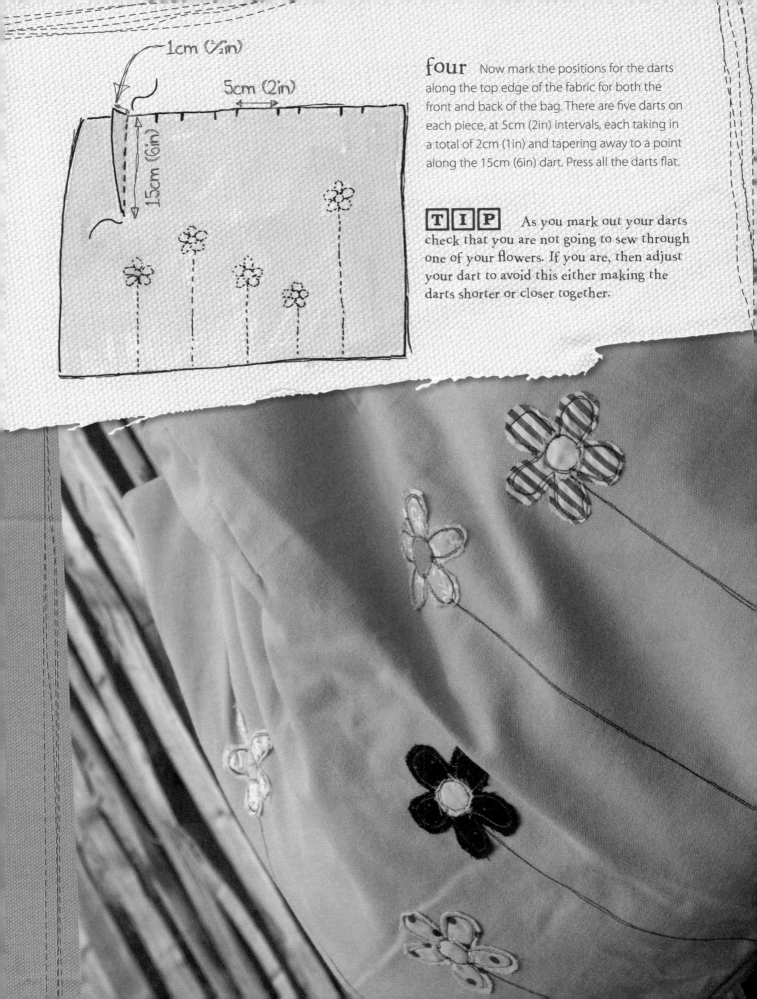

1cm (½in)

5cm (2in)

15cm (6in)

four Now mark the positions for the darts along the top edge of the fabric for both the front and back of the bag. There are five darts on each piece, at 5cm (2in) intervals, each taking in a total of 2cm (1in) and tapering away to a point along the 15cm (6in) dart. Press all the darts flat.

TIP As you mark out your darts check that you are not going to sew through one of your flowers. If you are, then adjust your dart to avoid this either making the darts shorter or closer together.

five Place each piece of bag fabric right sides together with a piece of lining. Trim the fabric pieces so that the width along the top edges is the same.

six Cut the tape into two lengths to make handles. Pin the ends of each handle between the lining and background pieces of the front and back of the bag. Insert one end of the tape close to the first dart and the other end close to the last dart. Sew along the top edge of both pieces, doubling back over the tape ends to make sure they are secure. Open the fabrics out and press the seams flat.

seven Place both pieces together, right sides facing, lining to lining and bag fabric to bag fabric. Sew all around the outer edges, leaving an opening in the bottom edge of the lining for turning.

tab pointing inward

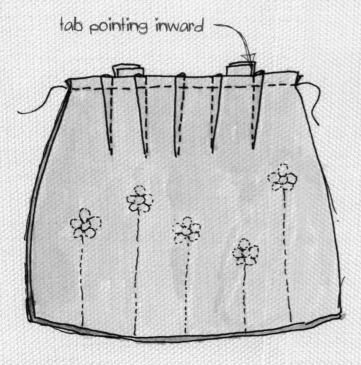

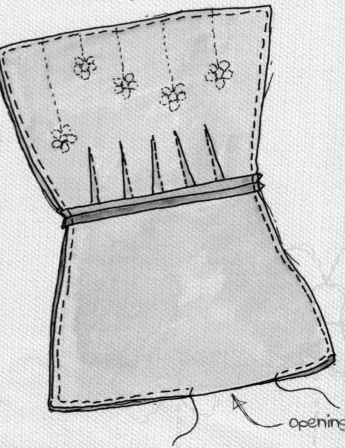

opening

eight Turn the bag right sides out. Press the edges of the opening in and then stitch it closed. Tuck the lining inside the main bag and you're ready to hit the shops.

T I P
You could add a pocket to your bag using the same method shown in the Whimsical Wall Tidy project (see page 66) and then you'll have somewhere for your purse, phone and keys.

call-off-the-search purse

How long do you spend rummaging in the depths of your bag looking for that illusive phone, pen, diary…? All those minutes a day probably add up to several hours a month and a few days a year. So it seems well worth spending a couple of hours making yourself these beautiful and oh-so-useful pouches to keep your belongings safely stowed away.

This simple little pouch with its colourful bunting closes with a lovely big button, but you can adapt the pattern to any number of uses by changing the size, fabrics and motif. By the time you're through with this project, you shouldn't lose anything ever again (hmmm, we'll see…).

hang out the bunting…fly the flag…

gather...

- 40 x 25cm (16 x 10in) of fabric for main pouch
- 40 x 25cm (16 x 10in) of fabric for lining
- Fabric for your chosen appliqué design
- Scraps of fabric to make a button loop
- Thread in various colours
- 60cm (24in) of narrow ribbon
- Large button

TIP Small pieces of background fabric may not fill the whole hoop, but try to keep the fabric as tight as possible.

one Trim your fabric for the main pouch and lining to the same size. Make a button loop of a size to accommodate your chosen button.

two Fold the main fabric into three sections for the front and back of the main pouch and the flap. Mark the fold lines on the wrong side. Decide where you want to place your appliqué design. For the bunting design, mark the position for the top line of the bunting on the flap and on the back of the pouch. Then sew two pieces of ribbon along each line, using straight stitch.

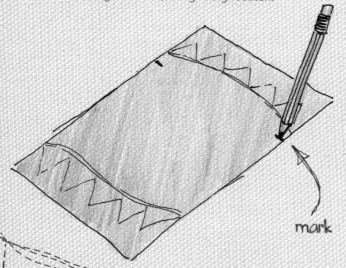

mark

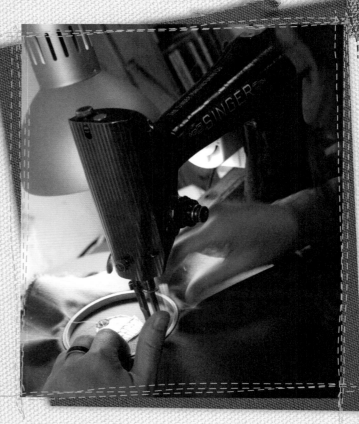

three Hoop up the fabric. Using the templates on page 126, cut out the appliqué pieces. Place them on the fabric below each line of ribbon, making sure they are within the seam allowance. Sew them in place by outlining (see pages 14–15). Trim all the loose threads and press.

tab pointing inward

four Place the lining and main fabrics right sides facing. Sew them together from one end of the flap fold to the other end of the flap fold, inserting your button loop as you go. (See page 45 on how to make the loop.) Don't forget that the folded end of the loop should point inward as the pouch is currently inside out.

five Sew the other end of the main and lining fabrics together.

six Open out the two pieces of fabric so that the main fabric is facing main fabric and the lining fabric is facing lining fabric, right sides together and with the flap uppermost. Carefully cut along the fold in the lining fabric, making sure there is an equal amount of fabric on each side of the cut.

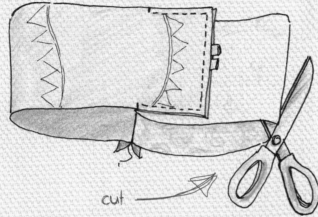

cut

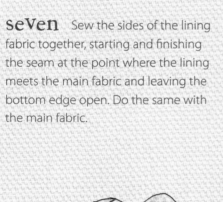

TIP Trim off the corners at an angle as you go to avoid excess bulk when you turn the work the right sides out.

seven Sew the sides of the lining fabric together, starting and finishing the seam at the point where the lining meets the main fabric and leaving the bottom edge open. Do the same with the main fabric.

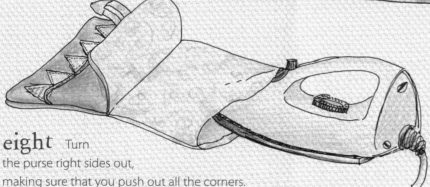

eight Turn the purse right sides out, making sure that you push out all the corners. Press in the edges of the opening on the lining fabric. Then sew up the opening with a matching colour of thread. Push the lining into the purse.

nine Finish your purse by stitching a dramatic button in place, taking care that it fits the button loop and that you sew it on firmly in the right position.

ALL AT SEA

This pattern is so versatile – create a purse of any dimension and add your own twist with different motifs (see page 126). Make it tiny for small change or sleek for sunnies. Attach a strap to fit around your wrist or across your body for an instant bag. The finished size of the small purse is 17 x 9.5cm (6½ x 3¾in) and 24.5x 10cm (9½ x 4in) for the long, thin purse.

perfect pinny and hairband

Once you've made this lovely apron you can wear it whilst you make one for each of your best friends, who are bound to want one as soon as they see it. Designed to look much more difficult than it is, the trick with this project is to really go for it when you choose and coordinate your fabrics.

A simple hairband completes the look.

I chose a palette of greens and blues, set off by a dark blue binding, for my apron. My favourite cup cake motif had to take the star turn here to inspire me to get into the kitchen more often to do a little baking! Maybe when I grow up I'll be a domestic goddess ...

kitchen goddess...

for the apron, gather...

- 100 x 80cm (40 x 32in) of cotton fabric for the main apron
- 30 x 25cm (12 x 10in) x 2 of contrasting fabric for the projects
- 1m (1yd) of bias binding
- Fabric for your chosen appliqué design
- 2m (2yd) of wide tape or ribbon to make ties
- Thread in various colours

T I P Think of a colour palette for your project – this makes it easier to find harmonious and accent colours for your appliqué.

one Make a paper pattern for the pocket, using the template on page 127. Cut two pieces, with fabric right sides facing, for the pockets.

two Cut out the pieces for your appliqué design, using the template on page 124 for the cup cake if you wish. Sew them in position, adding detail to show the flutes on the paper cases (see page 27). Trim the thread ends and press the pocket pieces.

three Place the pocket pieces wrong sides facing. Press the bias binding in half along its length. Pin and sew the binding to the curved edge of each pocket, trimming the binding to leave short loose ends.

four Press under the bottom and longer side edges of each pocket.

five Lay the fabric for the apron out flat and position the pockets so that the top and outer edges are flush with the edges of the apron fabric. Pin and sew them in place along the bottom and inner edges, leaving the top and outside edges open.

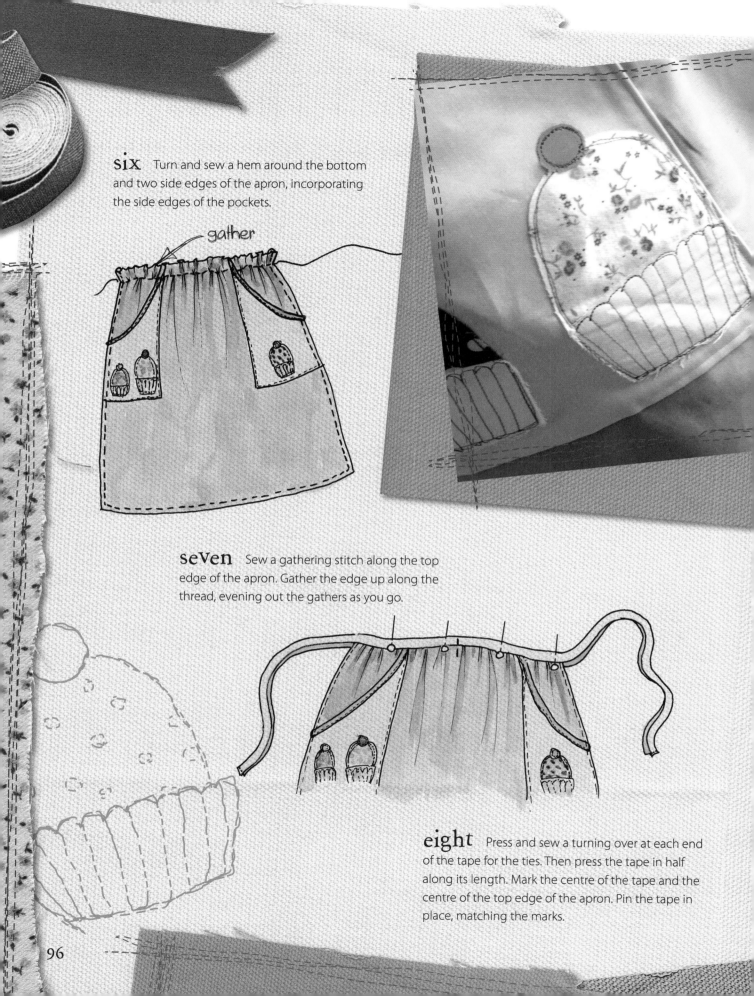

six Turn and sew a hem around the bottom and two side edges of the apron, incorporating the side edges of the pockets.

gather

seven Sew a gathering stitch along the top edge of the apron. Gather the edge up along the thread, evening out the gathers as you go.

eight Press and sew a turning over at each end of the tape for the ties. Then press the tape in half along its length. Mark the centre of the tape and the centre of the top edge of the apron. Pin the tape in place, matching the marks.

nine Sew along the entire length of tape, stitching the long edges together and sandwiching the gathered edge of the apron. Press your apron and start thinking about getting the recipe book out!

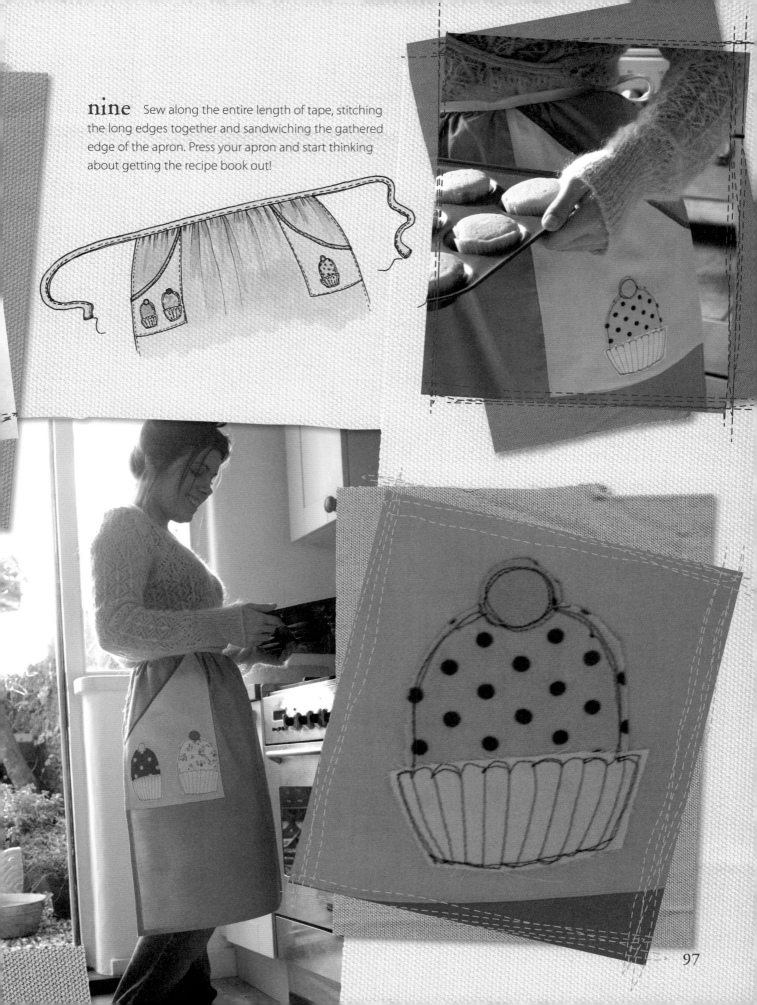

for the hairband, gather...

- 60 x 12.5cm (24 x 5in) of fabric for the hairband
- 60 x 12.5cm (24 x 5in) of lining fabric
- 15cm (6in) of wide elastic
- Fabric for your chosen appliqué design
- Threads in various colours

one Make a paper pattern using the template on page 127. Use this to cut out one piece of fabric for the hairband and a second for the lining. Transfer the marks for positioning the elastic to the wrong side of the hairband fabric.

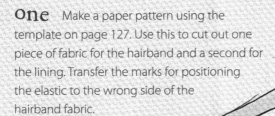

two Cut out the fabrics for your appliqué design, using the template on page 124 for the flower or your own ideas, as you wish. Outline your design (see pages 14–15), then trim the threads and press the fabric.

three Press a turning on both ends of the hairband and the lining fabrics. Place them right sides facing. Stitch along the front edge of the hairband, from one end to the other. Stitch along the back edge of the hairband starting and finishing at the marks for the elastic.

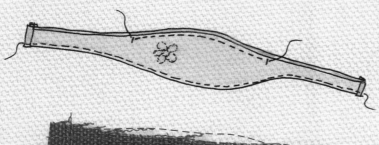

four Turn the hairband right sides out. Pin the ends of a length of elastic at the marks, so that it continues through the ends of the hairband and gathers the fabric up slightly.

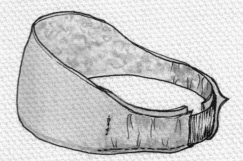

five Sew along the remaining back edge of the hairband, stretching the elastic as you do so. Hand stitch the two ends of the hairband together, taking care not to catch the elastic – and you're ready to sweep back your hair and get busy!

oh-so-tasty picnic blanket

This project is definitely a bit more of a challenge, but I really believe it's worth it. Inspired by beautiful patchwork quilts passed down through generations, it's my hope that this picnic blanket will help you create your very own family heirloom. The basic idea can easily be adapted to make oh-so-pretty napkins.

You can go as far as you want with this idea. You could keep it simple and embellish just one corner, or appliqué every last inch. You can combine lovely vintage fabrics and old clothes to embroider in your memories, or use shiny new fabrics knowing that the blanket will quickly gather its own history. Whatever you do, make sure you pack the ginger beer and cucumber sandwiches ... it's picnic time!

lashings of ginger beer...a breath of fresh air

for the blanket, gather…

- 1m (40in) of two fabrics for the blanket
- 50cm (20in) of two additional fabrics for the blanket
- 120 x 120cm (48 x 48in) of lining fabric
- 40 x 120cm (16 x 48in) of wide fabric for the binding
- Fabrics for your chosen appliqué design
- Threads in various colours

TIP For your blanket top, choose fabrics of a similar weight in contrasting patterns that look great together.

one Make a paper pattern, using the template on page 127. Cut out the four fabric pieces for the blanket top.

TIP It helps to cut out and assemble the blanket pieces on a big table or other flat surface – even a clean floor will do nicely.

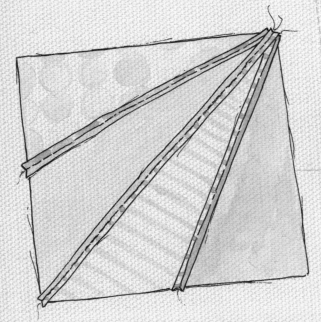

two Sew the blanket fabrics together to form a square. Press the back of the square, opening out the seams.

TIP This blanket gives you lots of space to play around with scale. Try repeating the same motif, making some shapes big and others small as I have done for the bumblebee motif – the results will always look great!

three Cut out the fabrics for your appliqué, using the template on page 124 for the bee and scaling up as desired. Outline the bees' stripy bodies onto your fabric (see pages 14–15). Add wings to your bees by outlining the shapes onto the blanket fabric and then shading them in with a pale-coloured thread (see pages 18–19). Trim the thread ends and press your design from the back.

four Cut the binding fabric into four equal 10 x 120cm (4 x 48in) strips. Press a turning around all four edges of the blanket top. Make a mark in each corner where the folds meet.

five Pin a strip of binding to each edge of the blanket top with an equal amount of loose binding at the ends. Sew the binding strips in place, starting and finishing at the corner marks and making sure you don't sew one strip to another. Open out the strips and press them flat, so that one end of each lies over its neighbour.

corner mark

six Mitre the corners of the binding, following the guidance on page 44–45. Trim any excess fabric and press the mitre seams open. Press the whole blanket top.

seven Place the blanket top and lining fabric together, right sides facing. Trim any excess fabric around the edges to make a perfect square. Then sew the two pieces together, leaving an opening in one side for turning. Trim the corners to reduce bulk (see page 44).

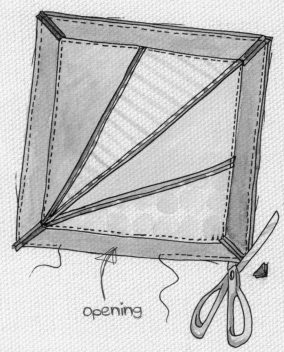

opening

eight Turn your blanket right sides out, press the turning on the opening and sew closed. Then head to the beach with a big basket full of scrumptious goodies!

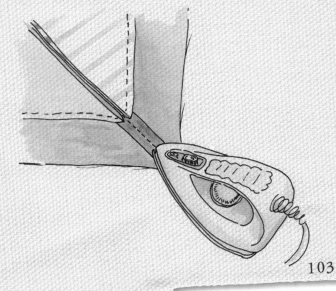

SITTING PRETTY

Adapt the blanket instructions to make pretty napkins for a perfect picnic. The finished napkins shown here measure approximately 80 x 80cm (31 x 31in). You could use the busy bee again, but the ladybird and butterfly motifs (see page 124 for the templates) will also ensure that those happy hours in glorious sunshine just flutter by. If you add wadding between the layers, you could also make a cot blanket or play mat for a baby – what a gorgeous gift!

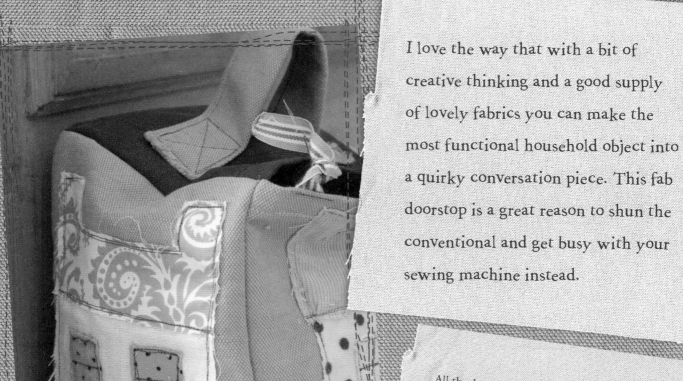

I love the way that with a bit of creative thinking and a good supply of lovely fabrics you can make the most functional household object into a quirky conversation piece. This fab doorstop is a great reason to shun the conventional and get busy with your sewing machine instead.

All the detail on this cute doorstop is in the appliqué and the choice of fabrics for the little houses. Once you've made your doorstop, it can be filled with dried rice or sand and popped next to your door to stop slamming, and encourage lots of great compliments!

another door opens...safe as houses...

gather...

- 60 x 20cm (24 x 5in) of heavyweight fabric for the sides
- 15 x 15cm (6 x 6in) x 2 of heavyweight fabric for the top and base
- 20 x 7.5cm (8 x 3in) of heavyweight fabric for the handle
- Fabric for your chosen appliqué design
- 50cm (20in) of ribbon for closing ties
- Threads in various colours
- A zip-lock bag of sand or rice

one Make a paper pattern for the houses, using the template on page 127. Cut out the fabric for your four little houses, choosing the colours carefully and making each house different.

two Fold the background fabric in half widthways and then half again. Press the folds to leave crease marks.

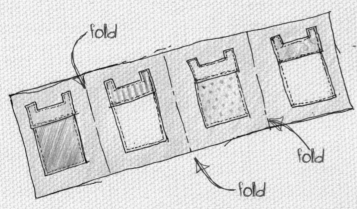

three Unfold and place the fabric pieces so that one house is centred on each of the four sections of side fabric. Outline each of the house and roof combinations in place on the background fabric (see pages 14–15), using contrasting colours of thread.

T I P Stitching twice around each piece ensures that they are well secured, and gives an extra 'sketchy' finish.

four Now appliqué on the windows and doors, using contrasting thread colours. Don't forget to add details like the windowpanes. Once your houses are appliquéd, trim the thread ends, cut the background fabric into four equal pieces and press.

five Make a fabric handle (see page 46). Centre and stitch the tab securely, using a square and cross formation, onto the fabric for the top of the doorstop.

insert

six Divide the ribbon into four equal lengths. Sew a hem along the back edge of the fabric for the top of the doorstop, attaching the ends of two lengths of ribbon as you go. Then repeat the process, this time along the top edge of the piece of appliquéd fabric that will make the back panel of the doorstop. Make sure the positions of the two pairs of ribbons match from one panel to the other.

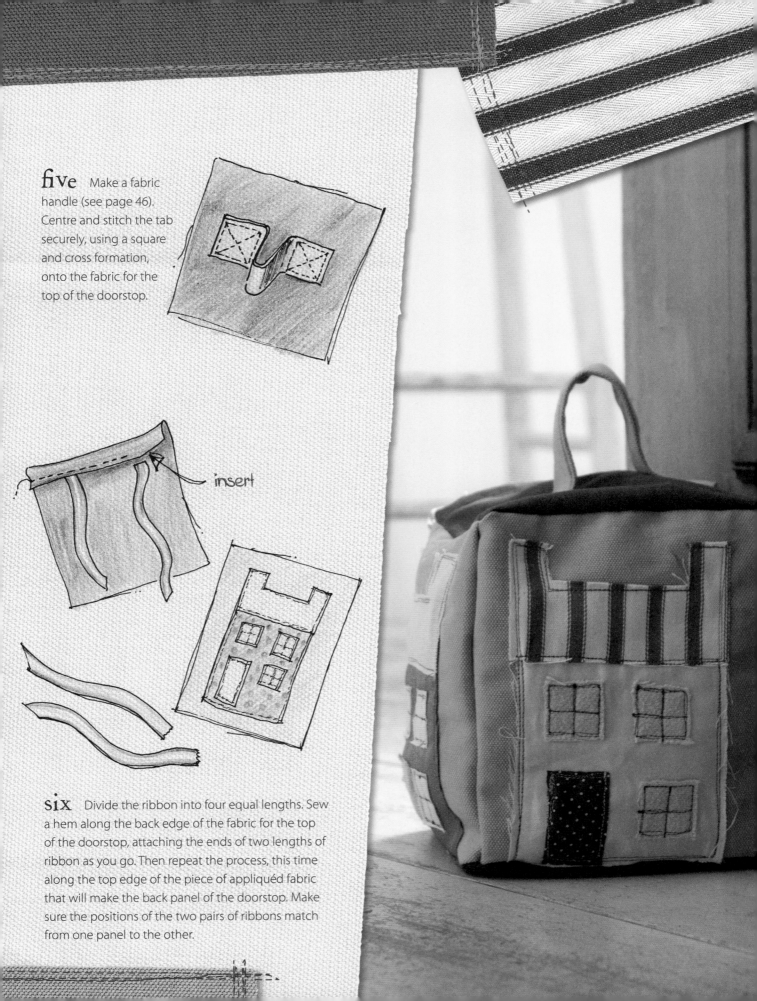

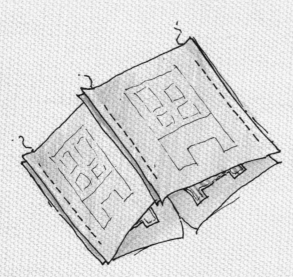

seven With right sides facing, sew together the four house panels, ensuring the bottoms of the panels are level with each other. Start the seams 1.5cm (⅝in) in from the top and bottom edges to make it easier to attach the remaining panels later.

eight With right sides facing, sew the bottom panel of fabric to the bottom edges of the four appliquéd panels.

nine Attach the top panel of fabric to the top edges of the appliquéd panels in the same way, but leaving the edge with the ribbon ties open. Turn your doorstop right sides out.

ten Fill your doorstop with a bag of rice or sand, and secure with the ribbon ties. Sit back and enjoy the view through your open door!

AROUND THE HOUSE

Make a collection of these decorative doorstops in different colours and sizes so you have one for every room. They also make great gifts – you could even make a mini doorstop as a paperweight.

extra comfy cushions

Is your sofa looking a little bare and forlorn at the moment? It couldn't be easier to make cushion covers, so it's time to get busy. That way you'll definitely have stylish cushions, in any shape or size you want, to match your room – so much more satisfying than buying the same as everyone else!

Although these cushions are simple to create, you can make them really eye-catching by choosing beautiful fabrics in gorgeous colours for any number of pretty motifs. I kept the cushion covers themselves quite plain so that the appliqué stands out, but you could make them quite exotic so that the motifs flit in and out of patterned backgrounds.

sitting pretty...home is where the heart is

gather...

- About 50cm (20in) of background fabric for each cushion
- About 50cm (20in) of backing fabric for each cushion
- Fabric for your chosen appliqué design
- Threads in various colours
- 1 cushion pad for each cushion

one To make a square cushion cover, cut out a square of the background fabric to match the size of your cushion pad, adding 5cm (2in) all around. Cut out a rectangle of fabric for the cushion backing by adding 20cm (8in) to one dimension of the original square. Now fold the backing fabric in half at right angles to the longest sides and cut along the fold.

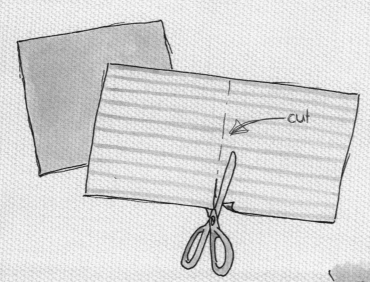

cut

two Cut out the fabric pieces for your chosen appliqué. The templates for the butterfly are on page 124 and should be scaled up x 2 for this project, but you could choose any of the others or design your own.

three Outline each fabric shape two or three times to attach it to the background fabric (see pages 14–15). You may need to hold the tips of the wings in place with a pin. Fill the body with a pale-coloured thread and the antennae with a carefully chosen accent colour, using the shading technique (see pages 18–19). Trim the thread ends and press the motif and background fabric.

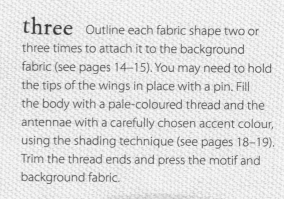

T I P These cushions are so versatile and easy to make you could make some fun-coloured cushions for a child's room or huge ones for a play area.

four Press and sew a hem along the two edges, one on each piece of backing fabric, that will eventually overlap each other to make an opening for the cushion pad. Place the background fabric face up on a flat surface. Then place first one, then the other, backing piece face down on the background fabric so that the two hemmed ends overlap. Pin the pieces in place.

five Sew around the entire outside edge of the cushion cover, doubling back over the points where the two lining pieces meet to make sure they are firmly secured. Trim any excess fabric from around the edges and cut across the corners to avoid them being too bulky (see page 44).

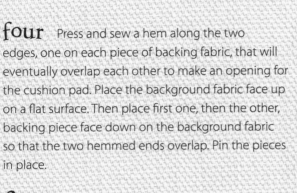

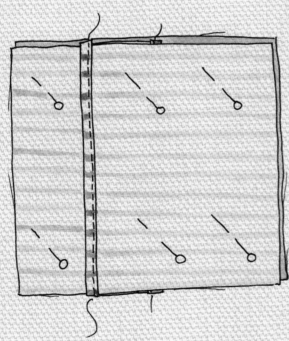

six Turn your cushion cover right sides out, stuff in your pad and get comfy on the sofa – you deserve a break!

FLUTTER ON BY

You can even make round cushions using the same method. Overlap the backing fabric to make an opening in the same way – you'll just need to sew the final seam around in a circle and trim away more fabric.

fresh-as-a-daisy curtains

If you're anything like me, the idea of making curtains is the sort of thing that makes you break out in a cold sweat! But do not fear – these charming little curtains are easy to make and look so pretty, you'll be wanting a house with more windows so you can dress them all!

Put the emphasis on bold colour and a striking design, and you definitely don't have to be a sewing diva to make these curtains. You just have to like buying fabulous fabric!

spring has sprung...busy as a bee...buzzz

gather...

- Curtain and lining fabric to suit the size of your window
- 30cm (12in) deep strip of fabric the same width as your curtains
- Fabric for your chosen appliqué design
- Threads in various colours
- About 1.5m (60in) of wide tape, depending on your curtain pole

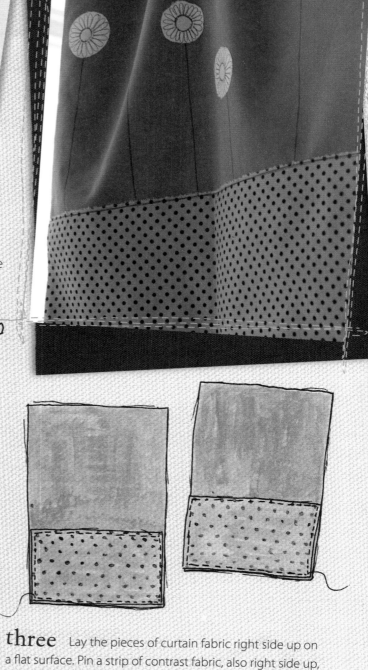

one Measure your window. Add extra to the length for the drop from tabs hanging from the curtain pole, any overhang below the windowsill and the top and bottom hems. Add extra to the width to allow for any extra fullness you might want, any overlap of the wall down the sides of the window and four side hems. Divide your measurements for the width in half to give you the dimensions of fabric for each curtain.

two Use your measurements to cut a piece of top fabric for each curtain. Cut two pieces of lining the same size. Cut the tape into five 15cm (6in) pieces for each curtain.

three Lay the pieces of curtain fabric right side up on a flat surface. Pin a strip of contrast fabric, also right side up, across the bottom of each piece, making sure they also lie perfectly flat. Using straight stitch, sew around each fabric strip at least twice to make sure they are well secured.

four Cut out the fabric pieces for your daisies and bees, using the templates on pages 124–125. The bee template should be scaled down x 1 so that it is in scale with the daisy. Arrange the shapes to make the most pleasing combination on your curtain pieces. Pin to hold them in place if you wish.

five　Outline the daisy heads and bees in position (see pages 14–15). Don't forget to add lots of petals for each daisy flower. Change to the running foot and straight stitch the daisy stems down to the contrast strip in a colour that contrasts well with the curtain fabric. Shade in the bee stripes with a dark-coloured thread and the bee wings with a pale-coloured thread (see pages 18–19). Trim the ends of thread and press the appliqué.

six　Fold over and press the seam allowance on all four sides of each curtain. Fold the lengths of tape in half and pin five at equal intervals on the right side along the top edge of each curtain. Remember that the ends should point towards the edge. Sew the tape in place to make the hanging tabs.

seven　Place your pieces of lining fabric, right sides up on a flat surface. Place the appliquéd curtain pieces, right sides down, on top. Make sure all the fabric is perfectly flat and pin around all the edges. Sew each curtain to its lining, leaving an opening for turning in each bottom edge. Trim the seams and corners to reduce bulk.

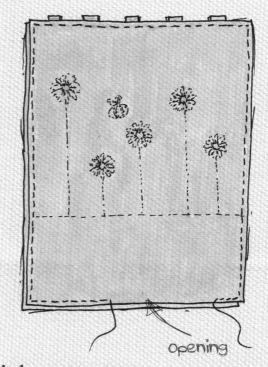

opening

T I P　Make the designs on your curtains asymmetrical, like mine, to add interest. Small children will love counting the daisies and spotting the bees.

eight　Turn your work right sides out, stitch the openings closed and find someone with good DIY skills to put up a pole so you can enjoy your curtains!

Templates

You will find the templates you need for the projects and appliqué motifs on the following pages. Make sure you enlarge them as advised either on the template or in the project instructions. If no enlargement figure is given, use the templates actual size.

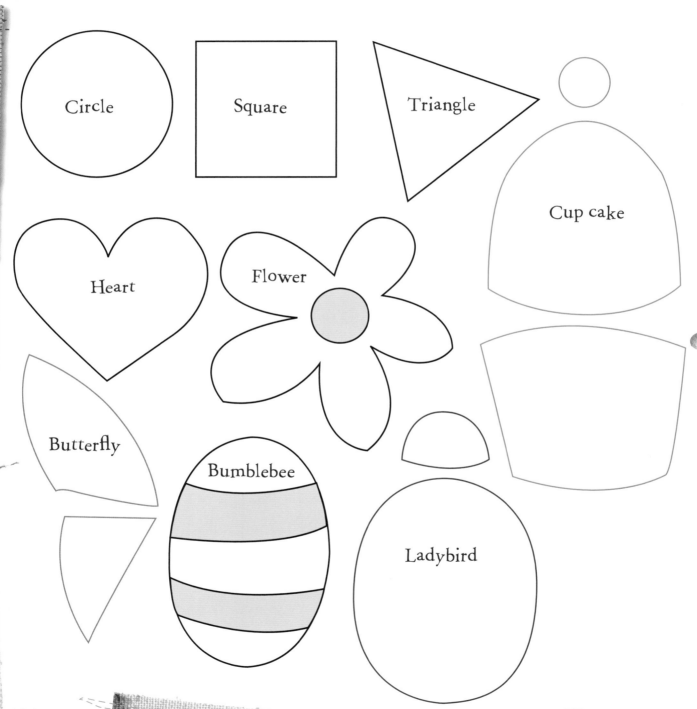

Circle

Square

Triangle

Cup cake

Heart

Flower

Butterfly

Bumblebee

Ladybird

Bow

Daisy

Aeroplane

Lily petal
Cut 5

Bell

Carrot

Tomato

Egg plant

Apple

Pea

Banana

Coffee cosy
Scale up x 2

Heart

Egg

Coffee cup
Scale up x 2

Egg cosy
Scale up x 2

Chick

Lifebuoy

Bunting

Boat

Scale up x 2

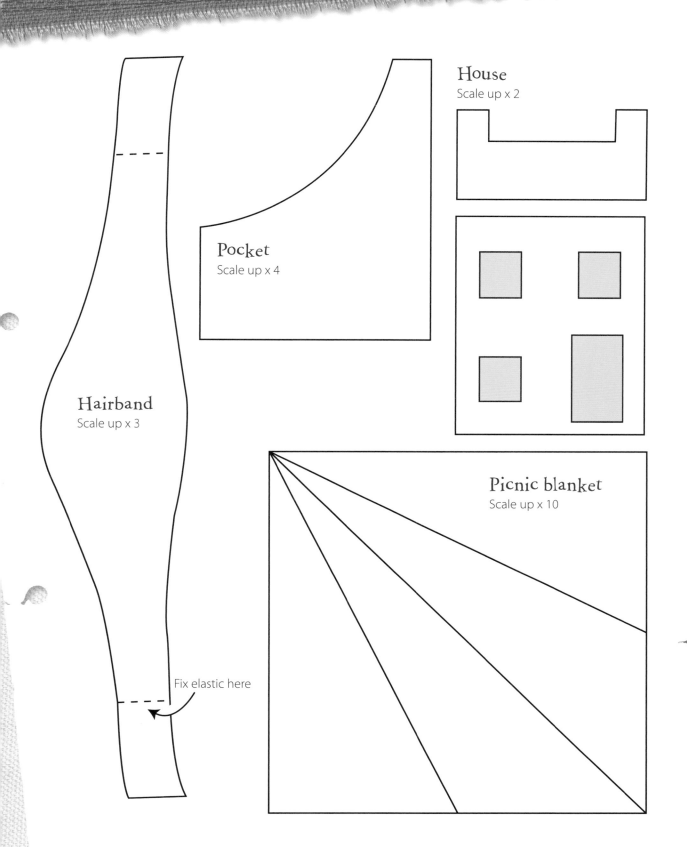

House
Scale up x 2

Pocket
Scale up x 4

Hairband
Scale up x 3

Picnic blanket
Scale up x 10

Fix elastic here

Suppliers

Here are some ideas for reliable suppliers of fabric, thread, trimmings and tools, but you will also find that your local vintage and thrift stores are great places to scavenge for the most gorgeous old fabrics, buttons and trimmings.

BASED IN THE USA
Great for discount fabrics
www.fabric.com
Great all round fabric supplier
JoAnn Fabrics at www.joann.com
Great for chintz, dots and stripes
www.reprodepot.com

BASED IN THE UK
For great fabrics, buttons, trimmings
Truro Fabrics, Lemon Quay, Truro, Cornwall TR1 2LW
Tel: 01872 222130
www.shop.trurofabrics.com

For lovely furnishing fabrics
Cotton Mills, Peoples Palace, Pydar St, Truro, Cornwall TR1 2AZ
Tel: 01872 278545

For a stunning range of threads
Calico Laine, 16 Liscard Crescent, Liscard, Wirral CH44 1AE
Tel: 0151 336 3939
www.calicolaine.co.uk

For a massive range of trimmings
Barnett Lawson Trimmings Ltd, 16–17 Little Portland Street, London W1W 8NE
Tel: 0207 636 8591
www.bltrimmings.com

For quality embroidery hoops
Tandem Cottage Needlework Ltd, PO Box 40, Glossop, Derbyshire SK13 1FB, UK
Tel: 01457 862610
www.tandem-cottage.co.uk

For scissors and other equipment
Morplan, 56 Great Titchfield Street, London W1W 7DF
Tel: 0207 636 1887
www.morplan.com

Acknowledgments

Many thanks to Freya Laughton and Becky Chard for helping me to devise the projects and to my sister Faye for manning the phone and running the business whilst putting up with me shouting 'I'm working on my book!'

About the author

Poppy Treffry runs her own textiles company based in Newlyn, Cornwall in the far south-west of England. She sells her quirky range of home furnishings, handbags and accessories all over the UK, the US and Europe, and has recently designed and made tea and coffee cosies for all the rooms at Claridges Hotel in London.

Poppy works on ancient Singer sewing machines, using simple techniques and a great eye for colour and pattern to create products that make people smile. She lives in Penzance with her partner, jeweller Justin Duance. They are just getting to know their first daughter Biba May, who was born in March 2009.

Index